Meditations in Revelation

Fifty-two exercises for
spiritual growth
from the
Revelation of Jesus Christ

By Jerry L. Marchbanks

Express Press, Lima, Ohio

MEDITATIONS IN REVELATION

PUBLISH MY WORD

FIRST EDITION
Copyright © 2002 by
Jerry L. Marchbanks

Library of Congress Catalog Card Number: 2002106986

Scripture quotations are from the *King James Version of the Bible*, in the public domain.

ISBN 0-7880-2055-2   PRINTED IN U.S.A.

*Blessed is he that readeth,
and they that hear the words of this prophecy,
and keep those things which are written therein:
for the time is at hand.   Rev 1:3*

CONTENTS

FOREWORD

Why Meditate in Revelation?

The book of Revelation may be one of the least read and most interpreted books of the Bible. Almost every day a new publication or article reports on the meaning of its mysterious symbolism. Many popular speakers and authors give the future some sense of immediacy by interpreting symbolism in current events. In my lifetime I have heard Hitler, Stalin, the Pope and Henry Kissinger, among several others, called the antichrist. Fictional accounts of an imminent future based on Revelation have become popular among both Christian and secular readers. The *Left Behind* series by Tim LaHaye and Jerry Jenkins draws adult followers much like the *Harry Potter* series does children. It is good to see such an interest in spiritual matters but a shame to see scriptural truth popularized through interpreters, rather than a reading of the book itself.

Revelation opens by immediately declaring a blessing to anyone who reads, hears and keeps its words. Still, the seemingly obscure images and text keep us away from the depth of its content. Several of my Christian friends tell me they don't read Revelation because it's hard to understand. We would rather read intriguing gospel stories, the rich prose of Paul's letters, or the beautiful poetry in Psalms. When it comes to Revelation, we often prefer reading what others think or imagine. As a result, we miss the promised blessing and risk being mislead into erroneous meanings.

Rather than depend on others, God wants us to personally experience the promised blessing of the book which identifies itself as the Revelation of Jesus Christ. It is a revelation, and by its own definition, the book can be read, understood and lived. The book of Proverbs also describes a threefold progression—knowledge, understanding and wisdom—which are parallel to the three steps of blessing promised in Revelation. Reading is an exercise that will lead to knowledge. Hearing implies understanding, and one of the best exercises for hearing is meditation. Having read and heard, we can exercise wisdom in obedient keeping of the words. Reading, hearing and keeping presses us toward another, perhaps more valuable attribute of Scripture, discovering and applying its truth in life today. Peter encourages us to "grow in grace, and in the knowledge of our Lord and Savior Jesus Christ" (2 Pet 3:18). Revelation may be cloaked in imagery, but it is clear about the nature of Jesus Christ: after all, it is *his* Revelation.

One reason many avoid the book of Revelation is because it is generally perceived as a prophetic rather than a spiritual book. In reality, most of Scripture is prophetic and some is as mysterious as Revelation. An early commentary on the book of Revelation by Matthew Henry includes the following statement about understanding its message:

> It is called the Revelation, because God therein discovers those things which could never have been sifted out by the reasonings of human understanding, those deep things of God which no man knows, but the Spirit of God, and those to whom he reveals them.

Matthew Henry understands revelation is a spiritual issue. As such, we must recognize the role of the Holy Spirit in helping us move from reading to understanding. Meditation is one of the most effective ways of allowing God's Holy Spirit to give life to Scripture. Read to gain knowledge; meditate to hear and gain understanding. Then take the step which understanding makes possible; keep the Word in the exercise of obedience—that is wisdom.

I have heard wisdom defined as an uncommon sense of common sense. It is a clever saying but scriptural wisdom does not really involve common sense. Godly wisdom is rooted in the Word of God and uncommonly revealed by the Holy Spirit. Wisdom becomes a reality by living out the uncommon truth of God's Word.

O how love I thy law!
it is my meditation all the day.

Thou through thy commandments
hast made me wiser than mine enemies:
for they are ever with me.

I have more understanding than all my teachers:
for thy testimonies are my meditation.

I understand more than the ancients,
because I keep thy precepts.

Ps 119:97-100

INTRODUCTION

The Blessing of Meditation

This book of the law shall not depart out of thy mouth; but thou shalt meditate therein day and night, that thou mayest observe to do according to all that is written therein: for then thou shalt make thy way prosperous, and then thou shalt have good success.   *Josh 1:8*

There are many spiritual disciplines advocated in Scripture and even more are often promoted within individual churches. Disciplines advocated in Scripture are often multi-faceted and almost always include a promise of specific blessing. Meditation is one of the richest disciplines, perhaps exceeded in promised blessing only by the admonition to pray.

One frequently encouraged discipline is fasting, but unless it is accompanied by prayer, fasting is just dieting. Prayer and fasting are often mentioned as a couplet in scripture. Memorization is another commonly promoted spiritual discipline, one which amazingly, finds little support in Scripture. Memorization is encouraged as a way to hide the Word in your heart and a way to keep from sin (Psalm 119:11). Unfortunately, memorization without meditation may be just rote; alone, it is storing words in your mind, not your heart. Meditation is the way to the heart and out of the heart we can choose wisdom.

Let the words of my mouth, and the meditation of my heart, be acceptable in thy sight, O LORD, my strength, and my redeemer.   *Ps 19:14*

The blessings of meditation are not general. God has given specific promises and tied them directly to consistent practice of meditation.

How would you like to lead a life characterized by the following qualities?

- A Prosperous Way
- Good Success
- Delight in the Lord
- Vibrant Prayer
- A Satisfied Soul
- A Love for Scripture

- A Desire to Obey God
- Knowing the Fear of God
- Understanding the Ways of God
- Positive Life Attitude
- Sound Sleep and Rest
- Wisdom and Understanding

Try meditation. These are a few of the blessings which Scripture associates with this dynamic spiritual discipline. God asks us, commands us, to meditate on his Word. King David loved to meditate; his psalms focus on the practice of meditation and identify a host of resulting blessings. The most frequent mention of meditation is in Psalm 119, a Psalm of 176 verses and every verse mentions the Word of God.

Even new age thinking recognizes the power of meditation because it roots in our heart and gives life to whatever it is focused upon, even ungodly ways. Bookstores dedicate ample shelve-space to the subject and Internet sites abound. Special "spiritual centers" exist which promote the discipline as a way of life. The counterfeit produces it's promised peace, but God has a better way—meditate on his Word.

The purpose of this book is to approach Revelation as a meditative writing. For this reason, little attempt is given to interpretation of prophetic imagery. Rather, the emphasis is on verses that speak to our heart and enable us to practice its wisdom in daily life.

There are many forms of meditation, some of which are discussed in the appendix of this book. The approach used here is meditation on a verse within the context of a passage. This is probably the most common form of biblical meditation. It allows for focused and personal reflection within the context of a broader passage. Following this method, Revelation is read, passage by passage, and the Word is heard through meditation and reflection. The natural result should be to keep the truth meditation places in our heart.

To make meditation practical this book advocates a form of journaling. Journaling is another highly promoted spiritual discipline which, like the others, requires spiritual input. Journaling without meditation may just be keeping a diary. A diary may have value, but a journal of meditations will document our experience with the living God. It will not be a book that needs to be locked up, as a diary often is, but a book that speaks words of truth through our life.

> *Meditate upon these things; give thyself wholly to them; that thy profiting may appear to all. Take heed unto thyself, and unto the doctrine; continue in them: for in doing this thou shalt both save thyself, and them that hear thee.*
> *1 Tim 4:15-16*

The approach to journaling personal meditations represent my own reading, hearing and keeping of the words. They are presented as an offering to God and as an example for the readers personal use. My prayer is the Holy Spirit will use these words to encourage you to begin or deepen a contemplative life.

The meditations are presented in five parts, each designed to demonstrate a specific element of meditation and to uncover a spiritual element in the book.

Passage: A selected verse, or verse segment, is presented along with the passage from which it is drawn. This requires the passage, and ultimately the book, to be read. Mainly, it prevents meditating out of context, which can lead to as much error as reading out of context. I believe most biblical error comes from not considering context.

Context: A brief contextual discussion is presented. The purpose of meditation is not the same as bible study, so the study is brief. It is provided only to strengthen the principle of contextual meditation.

Prayer: Prayer is offered in the form of a letter to Jesus. Prayer and meditation go together. Prayer is the discipline that puts spiritual power behind meditation. We are not seeking our understanding; that would be common sense.

We are seeking revelation through the Holy Spirit who speaks of Christ. Writing a letter to Jesus allows us to use a journaling approach in meditation.

Reflection: What do you hear in the words? The process is to move from reading to hearing which gives understanding. Reflection is writing down what we hear, not just the words, but the revelation.

Practice: Read, hear and keep—finally, we must do something with the revelation to give it life. Practice is recording a choice or a decision that results from understanding. It is wisdom to be exercised. It is defining what the revelation looks like in life. It is to answer the question posed by Francis Schaeffer in his classic book, *How Should We Then Live?*

This book of meditations in Revelation includes fifty-two meditations. They were originally done as my own daily meditations. Perhaps it is not a coincidence that there are fifty-two meditations, one for each week in a year. God has something special to say about a week. It was his time for creation and the time basis for many biblical events. Weeks are referred to in many of the prophetic passages.

In view of this God-incidence, consider using these meditations on a weekly basis. Begin the week with the meditation and focus on its various elements during the days of the week.

In the book's Appendix there is a discussion of various approaches to meditation, including a discussion of word by word meditation. Begin the week with the passage-verse meditation and select words of the verse and apply word by word meditation during the week. The last day of the week should focus on reflection—let the Holy Spirit bring it all together on that day.

Do not neglect the practice suggestions. A week will give opportunity for the exercises to begin to become habit.

The first meditation suggests you speak the name of Jesus in public once every day. Commit to it for a week; see what happens.

Finally, be expectantly prepared for the blessings which God has promised through meditation.

Blessed is the man
that walketh not in the counsel of the ungodly,
nor standeth in the way of sinners,
nor sitteth in the seat of the scornful.

But his delight is in the law of the LORD;
and in his law doth he meditate day and night.

And he shall be like a tree planted by the rivers of water,
that bringeth forth his fruit in his season;
his leaf also shall not wither;
and whatsoever he doeth shall prosper.

Ps 1:1-3

1. A Living Witness

Who bare record of the word of God, and of the testimony
of Jesus Christ, and of all things that he saw.   Rev 1:2

CONTEXT

The Revelation of Jesus Christ, which God gave unto him,
to shew unto his servants things which must shortly come
to pass; and he sent and signified it by his angel unto his
servant John: **Who bare record of the word of God, and**
of the testimony of Jesus Christ, and of all things that he
saw. *Blessed is he that readeth, and they that hear the*
words of this prophecy, and keep those things which are
written therein: for the time is at hand.   *Rev 1:1-3*

In many ways the whole of Scripture is a revelation of Jesus
Christ. This final book in the sacred text declares itself to be just
that and pronounces a blessing for those who will read, hear and
keep its words.

It is important to always remember the book is a revelation.
Although it is filled with mysterious images and symbolism, it
should not be a mystery to servants of Jesus Christ who diligently
seek to understand.

To others the words will always be a mystery because its revelation is spiritual, given through the Holy Spirit, who speaks of
Jesus. When Jesus walked the earth he spoke in parables which
were given for the believers edification. Asked why he spoke in
parables, Jesus replied: "Therefore speak I to them in parables:
because they seeing see not; and hearing they hear not, neither do
they understand" (Matt 13:13). The words read, hear and keep
take on even more significance when viewed in this light. The
mystery fades and the symbolism opens, as we begin to see and
experience a new vision of the person of our Lord and Savior, Jesus
the Christ.

There is much to think about in this opening passage. Surely the admonition to read, hear and keep needs to be written in our heart and applied throughout all of our meditations. However, the fruit of our meditation is to be a testimony of Jesus. Our own lives will testify of him if we call ourselves his servants. We may be all of Jesus someone ever sees.

The thing to consider in this meditation is how we individually bear record of the living word in our own lives. If we read, hear and keep the words, then we can become the revelation of Jesus Christ. The question always will remain, will our revelation of him be true to the truth?

There is a sense of urgency, the passage closes by pointing out, *for the time is at hand.* Timing is always critical in the plan of God. Jesus did not rush to the cross, neither did he avoid it when his time was fully come (John 7:8). In like manner, we need to wait on God's timing for most things. However, in the matter of reading, hearing and keeping the words of this book, God declares the time to be at hand.

Now, today, is the fullness of time for salvation and for the knowledge of God in Christ.

Dear Lord Jesus

This is a glorious calling, Lord. It needs to be the essence of my life and all the ways I express life in word and deed. My testimony needs to be based firmly on Scripture, testify of you and be expressed in the practicality of things I see in daily life. Praise to you, Lord, for the scriptures. Praise to the Father for giving you, his only Son, for my salvation. Thank you, Lord, for making it all imminently practical in life today. You are Lord of creation and Lord of eternity. For me you are Lord of today. I am blessed to have a word of testimony, the hope of greater testimony, and a life which can testify of your abundant love for today.

Your record bearer.

REFLECTION

John bore record of the word of God and of what he saw. I think this means he wrote it down. John wrote what he saw as it reflected God's word and the testimony of Christ, the Lord. These two are obviously consistent because Christ is the Word. I can also write it down and that is the challenge for today. John wrote as the Holy Spirit made revelation occur. I pray for spiritual direction and words, so that what I write will have life. I want to reflect words of the Spirit so they will be truth and a testimony of Christ living in me in a practical way. Praise to my Savior whose word is life.

PRACTICE

One of the toughest issues in our Christian walk is how to be a living witness. If we are not careful, trying to be a living witness can wear us out. Big words like evangelism, service and ministry will draw us into a frenzy of activity as we strive to be an effective witness for Christ. Perhaps one approach is not to strive, but listen and do those things he calls us to. That is why we are called his servants—someone who does what his master desires.

Being a living witness implies doing something which others can see. If it cannot be seen, it is not alive. The light of Christ in our lives is not designed to be hidden.

> *Ye are the light of the world. A city that is set on an hill cannot be hid. Neither do men light a candle, and put it under a bushel, but on a candlestick; and it giveth light unto all that are in the house. Let your light so shine before men, that they may see your good works, and glorify your Father which is in heaven.* Matt 5:14-16

I think we can begin by seeing Christ in others, see his face in the face of others who believe. We may not be able to see Christ in the faces of those who have yet to believe, but we can see with eyes

19

of hope. We know God loves them and desires for them to enter into eternal life. In this light, our living witness becomes a calling. It is a calling to see the hope of Christ in every person and to let his love draw them toward the joy of salvation.

If we can see Christ, or the potential of Christ, in others we will serve them with God's love because we love him. Jesus said: "Inasmuch as ye have done it unto one of the least of these my brethren, ye have done it unto me" (Matt 25:40b).

The issue is not the service, but the love. Expressing godly love will not be burdensome. It may be hard and involve both weeping and mourning, but the result will be rest, not strife.

A popular song says they will know we are Christians by our love; but I think they will know it is the love of Christ by our testimony of him.

A good practice while meditating on being a living witness is to speak his name. Say the name of Jesus out loud every day. Say it so that someone can hear. Then it will be his testimony, not ours. He will draw those who will hear to himself. Our living witness is to speak his name and to love with his love.

---

2. A Living Body

> I John, who also am your brother, and companion in tribulation, and in the kingdom and patience of Jesus Christ, ...
>
> Rev 1:9a

CONTEXT

> *John to the seven churches which are in Asia: Grace be unto you, and peace, from him which is, and which was, and which is to come; and from the seven Spirits which are before his throne; And from Jesus Christ, who is the faithful witness, and the first begotten of the dead, and the prince of the kings of the earth. Unto him that loved us, and washed us from our sins in his own blood, And hath made us kings and priests unto God and his Father; to him be glory and dominion for ever and ever. Amen. Behold, he cometh with clouds; and every eye shall see him, and they also which pierced him: and all kindreds of the earth shall wail because of him. Even so, Amen. I am Alpha and Omega, the beginning and the ending, saith the Lord, which is, and which was, and which is to come, the Almighty.* **I John, who also am your brother, and companion in tribulation, and in the kingdom and patience of Jesus Christ,** *was in the isle that is called Patmos, for the word of God, and for the testimony of Jesus Christ.*   Rev 1:4-9

Virtually every epistle in the new testament opens with the pronouncement of grace and peace. They also point out grace and peace are from Jesus Christ and ministered through the Holy Spirit. Larry Crabb, a well known Christian author, says the two principle vacuums in life are significance and security. According to Sanford Williams, a less known but gifted teacher of the Word, grace and peace are God's provision for these areas of aloneness. We are only significant because of the grace of God and we find security only in the peace of God.

The phrase "which is, and which was, and which is to come" is used twice in this passage. These eternal qualities of our God remind us of the three things which Paul concludes to be permanent in I Corinthians 13—faith, hope and love. In a God "which is" we can experience his love today: it becomes our grace and peace. In a God "which was" we can experience his faith, not bound in regret but in the confidence of his grace. In a God "which is to come" we can experience his hope, not anxious over circumstances but resting in his peace.

It is the testimony of Jesus Christ, the faithful witness who declares the gospel. The good news of our salvation is found in him. It is he who loved us, and it is he who washed us from our sins in his own blood. To recognize the pain he suffered should cause us to wail; it was our sin he suffered and died for. Our mourning is turned to joy as we realize it was a gift of his love and has purchased our salvation—if we only believe.

John closes this salutation by identifying himself as our brother. We who are called by Jesus' name are called his body. In a very real sense we are one family and one in the unity of God's Holy Spirit. It is a unity which finds its perfection in diversity. Man's view of unity is often interpreted as sameness. The beauty of God's creation is what seems to be an infinite variety of beauty. All proclaiming unity as they fulfill their created purpose.

Let us meditate on the implications of being a part of the body of Christ, both in tribulation and in the joy of his kingdom.

Our living witness will be multiplied when it is expressed in a living body. The light of one candle is marvelous, but the light of many candles can enlighten the whole world with the possibility of salvation. When the light of God's truth is magnified in the body of Christ and focused by the power of his Holy Spirit, there will be a warmth of love to attract those whom he has called to the light.

The great commandment has become the great commission. We are called to love and to go and proclaim his love to the world. It cannot be done except as a living body—the body of Christ.

Dear Lord Jesus

Thank you, Lord, for the body of Christ, my companions and my strength; my encouragement and also my burden. We have tribulation in this world, but you have overcome and given me the strength to encourage and the patience to be encouraged. I am in your kingdom, even while living in this worldly domain of darkness. That is why patience is so important. I will see the fullness of your kingdom. The tribulation of this world will pass. The body of Christ will become what you have purposed it to be. In the meantime I can love you and my neighbor. I can love others with your love. I can live in your glory as a part of your body.

Glory and dominion to you.

REFLECTION

I am not alone. The Lord is good to have his body on this earth. I have companions in tribulation. I have a biological family to uphold me and a family in the Lord to correct, edify, encourage and enlighten me. Praise to our God who has not left us just to wait for his return. He has given us his Word and his Spirit. His Spirit binds us together in his kingdom. In it we can have his patience as we wait for the hope of his soon return. In the meantime, he is in our midst; and we can enjoy his love in the life of his body.

PRACTICE

To practice being a living body, we must begin by acknowledging the body of Christ is a reality. Jesus claims to be in our midst when we gather in his name (Matt 18:20). His presence in the midst of our lives together can be seen in a real and practical way. We are, in fact, the manifestation of his presence on this earth. Dare we treat it lightly?

When Jacob was reconciled to Esau after experiencing the bitterness and brokenness of deception, he made an interesting comment to Esau:

> *... for therefore I have seen thy face, as though I had seen the face of God, and thou wast pleased with me.*
>
> *Gen 33:10b*

The practice of being a living body is to see the face of Jesus in the face of other believers. This is not just seeing him in joyful countenances, but also in those that weep. The physical body of Christ was broken, and in many ways his spiritual body is broken today. Let us be healers by practicing the presence of God in our mutual lives.

Purpose to tell someone today, and everyday, that you see the face of Jesus in their face. Recognize that your countenance is a reflection of his image. Let the awareness of God's presence become a reality. His presence is real, and the blessing of recognizing it will amaze you.

---

3. A Living Hope

> Write the things which thou hast seen, and the things which
> are, and the things which shall be hereafter;   Rev 1:19

CONTEXT

*I was in the Spirit on the Lord's day, and heard behind me
a great voice, as of a trumpet, Saying, I am Alpha and
Omega, the first and the last: and, What thou seest, write
in a book, and send it unto the seven churches which are in
Asia; unto Ephesus, and unto Smyrna, and unto Pergamos,
and unto Thyatira, and unto Sardis, and unto Philadelphia, and unto Laodicea. And I turned to see the voice
that spake with me. And being turned, I saw seven golden
candlesticks; And in the midst of the seven candlesticks
one like unto the Son of man, clothed with a garment down
to the foot, and girt about the paps with a golden girdle.
His head and his hairs were white like wool, as white as
snow; and his eyes were as a flame of fire; And his feet like
unto fine brass, as if they burned in a furnace; and his
voice as the sound of many waters. And he had in his right
hand seven stars: and out of his mouth went a sharp
twoedged sword: and his countenance was as the sun
shineth in his strength. And when I saw him, I fell at his
feet as dead. And he laid his right hand upon me, saying
unto me, Fear not; I am the first and the last: I am he that
liveth, and was dead; and, behold, I am alive for ever-
more, Amen; and have the keys of hell and of death.* **Write
the things which thou hast seen, and the things which
are, and the things which shall be hereafter;** *The mystery
of the seven stars which thou sawest in my right hand, and
the seven golden candlesticks. The seven stars are the angels of the seven churches: and the seven candlesticks which
thou sawest are the seven churches.*   Rev 1:10-20

There is something special about the Lord's day. God gave us the day and told us to rest. Instead, the busyness of the world rushes us through the day and headlong into the next. We look forward to rest but it doesn't seem to come. John was in the Spirit on the Lord's day; it was a special attitude, one that allows the Lord of rest to speak to us in our spirit.

In the Spirit, John was overwhelmed by a vision of Jesus and fell at his feet as a dead man. Somehow we are all dead men except for the touch of our Lord and Savior. The words of Jesus were "Fear not," which are the first words in any visitation described in the Bible. But there is more—Jesus touched John and told him who he was. The entire vision is a revelation of Jesus Christ. His glory is shown in his righteousness, his power, his discernment, his judgement, and his authority. His touch brings his words to us personally. His words tell of his death, his eternal life and his authority over death and hell—of salvation.

When we hear from Jesus, our assurance also begins with "Fear not" and his comfort will be our salvation. We may sing "He Touched Me," but it will be a vision of his redemption that changes our lives. He died for me, a sinner with every reason to fear eternity. He arose and overcame death and hell so that I can "Fear not." His touch is the touch of eternity.

Dear Lord Jesus:

John saw you and fell at your feet, but you said "fear not" and told him to write. You said write about what was. Lord, that is the word of faith. You said write about what is. Lord, that is the word of love. You said write about what will be. Lord, that is the word of hope. Thank you Lord, for the fullness and permanence of things that remain: faith, hope and love. Help me to write about them Lord, but help me to write with the humility of knowing you and with the courage to fear not. You are beyond description, but you give us vision. Help me share it, Lord.

Writing.

REFLECTION

"Write," it was a word to John. Can I let it be a word for me? I know God has spoken to me in Scripture and in circumstance. The Holy Spirit has a way of speaking so that I, like John, can be in the Spirit. Oh, how much I want to hear in my spirit his words for me. Then I will know that God is in my works, and it is not just something for me to do. What do I know to be true and from the Lord? I know he has given me a heart and a mind for the Word. I know he has led me to principles that are life-changing and can affect the body of Christ. I may lack verbal skills and use immature writing skills, but God will not ask me to do what he will not enable. I can learn. He can teach. Praise his name!

PRACTICE

What is it that we fear? Psychologists identify myriads of phobia; many we can identify and even joke about. But God says "Fear not." He says we should not be anxious, but come to him in prayer and thanksgiving (Philippians 4:6). Talk to him about it, he is near, he has and will touch us. God says to cast our cares on him because he cares for us (1 Peter 5:7). These are great words of assurance and of comfort.

Why do we not do as he says? He has been, is and will be faithful. Somehow we treasure our anxieties as if they are part of our identity. Actually they are part of us—our old nature—that which needs to die so that our new nature can live.

It is not impossible to overcome fear and anxiety. God has given us the gift of faith, a vision of hope, and love to sustain us in the daily effort. Faith, hope and love: what was, what will be and what is. What have we to fear?

> *What shall we then say to these things? If God be for us, who can be against us?*   *Rom 8:31*

One thing we can know about hope, is it's not wishful thinking. Our salvation is real, God's promise of care is real and hope is a reality. The reality of hope may not resemble our wishes, but we can live in the knowledge that his ways are higher than ours. We can rest, knowing he loves us and see our future as good. Our hope is in Christ and our life is also in him. Of all people, we are the most hopeful.

John was told to write, and that is good medicine for us as well. When we write about the faithfulness of God we will be strengthened to "Fear not" when the next cause for anxiety arises. Also, writing seems to crystalize vague fears. It gives it an identity and definition. It is much easier to deal with specific issues: then we can pray clearly and recognize the grace of God as he quenches our fears with his perfect love.

Practice casting your cares on God by writing them down. Hold the paper up, give it to God. Later, look back and praise him for his faithfulness. Then hope will become living hope, firmly settled in his faithfulness.

---

4. Overcoming - Lost Love

He that hath an ear, let him hear what the Spirit saith unto the churches; To him that overcometh will I give to eat of the tree of life, which is in the midst of the paradise of God.
                                                                    Rev 2:7

CONTEXT

Unto the angel of the church of Ephesus write; These things saith he that holdeth the seven stars in his right hand, who walketh in the midst of the seven golden candlesticks; I know thy works, and thy labour, and thy patience, and how thou canst not bear them which are evil: and thou hast tried them which say they are apostles, and are not, and hast found them liars: And hast borne, and hast patience, and for my name's sake hast laboured, and hast not fainted. Nevertheless I have somewhat against thee, because thou hast left thy first love. Remember therefore from whence thou art fallen, and repent, and do the first works; or else I will come unto thee quickly, and will remove thy candlestick out of his place, except thou repent. But this thou hast, that thou hatest the deeds of the Nicolaitans, which I also hate. He that hath an ear, let him hear what the Spirit saith unto the churches; **To him that overcometh will I give to eat of the tree of life, which is in the midst of the paradise of God.**   *Rev 2:1-7*

Jesus is in the midst! He promised that where we gather together he would be the essence, or midst, of our gathering. Sometimes we use the presence of our Lord as a pressure to elicit good behavior from our children. It's a scary thing for a child to hear the words, "Jesus is watching every thing you do." Still, it is true. As adults we need to be more aware of our visibility before the Lord. It needn't be a scary thing, however; Jesus loves us and knows us.

A sense of his presence should be a comfort and encouragement to righteousness in life. The fear of God is real; but it should draw us to him for healing. Worldly fear makes us draw back; his fear draws us forward.

Jesus knows our good works and commends them, but his heart is directed toward our ways. He knows that without love all our good works are dead works. Good works may comfort, even heal, but without love they lose eternal value.

Leaving our first love is easier than we might think. The excitement of first love may contain the very seed for its own loss. We are this strange contradiction of treasure in an earthen vessel, jars of clay filled with the beauty of God's love. Unfortunately, excitement is an expression of the clay; while love is the essence of what the jar contains. How easily excitement passes. How critical it is for us to focus on the depth of love rather than the excitement of living.

Jesus's call is to repent, another hard choice. The passage reminds us that repentance involves remembering, turning and exercising godly choices. Somehow we must learn to recognize and hate evil. When we appreciate the horror of sin, the fear of God will compel us toward his love so godly choices can be made.

Overcoming may be making hard choices exercised in hard circumstances, but the result is worth it. The jar of clay can find life and live it in the midst of the kingdom of heaven. It is not a future promise it is near and present. Jesus is in the midst; and we can become in his midst. It's part of being conformed to his image.

Dear Lord Jesus:

The issue with Ephesus was "thou hast left thy first love." The solution was repentance and the promise was life. Praise you Lord, I know what it is to leave my first love, and I know what it means to fall. Praise to you Lord, I also know what it means to repent and experience the joy of your restoration. It's like recovering the blessing of my first love. Help me Lord, to do the first works, things that really matter in your kingdom. Help me Lord to live in the midst of your life and to be nourished with the tree of life and your Word. Help me Lord to share it in your body and in the world.

Overcoming.

REFLECTION

Overcoming is not easy, it is contrary to my flesh. The things of the flesh are easy but completely unfulfilling. I must overcome to live in the Spirit. In life there is something akin to the force of gravity; it is downward. In life, gravity comes from the fall and makes sin the downhill choice. Holiness is an uphill choice. I must choose not only to overcome the downhill pressure, I must choose to climb uphill. Praise to my God who strengthens me for the climb. On most days I like to go running. A nice easy jog to keep me fit, without hills, is not so bad. It takes a positive choice to do hard workouts or climb hills, but that is where gain occurs. Growth will come from pressing beyond our comfort zone in the flesh. Spiritual growth will come from making spiritual choices and expressing them in life.

PRACTICE

Jesus says he knows our works and counsels us to do the first works, the works of love. This book of Revelation opens with a blessing to those who read, hear and keep the words. Jesus reminds us repentance involves confession, remorse and new choices. Repentance is making the choice to overcome.

One of the real dangers of meditation is it may not germinate in the soil of life. Reading and hearing may not lead to keeping. The seed of God's word may never bear fruit. Meditation can be pleasant in itself. I find myself saying—isn't that nice, as an insight arises from a passage during my reflection. The test will come later in the day when an opportunity to exercise the principle arises. Too often, the moment passes and I remain unchanged, unresponsive to the truth meditation has planted in my heart. Good

31

seed planted in hard or rocky soil produces little or no fruit. What a loss that is to me, to others and to the kingdom of God.

God's word is not passive, it is active. It must find expression in life or it dies in the place it is planted. The Boy Scouts encourage a daily good deed. They may have it right, and we can learn to practice by choosing to find a way to do a good deed every day. Initially, these good deeds may be dead works; but as we meditate, the Holy Spirit will turn our heart toward love and our good deeds will become his good deeds, the works of God.

Practice overcoming by finding someone to bless every day. Let someone go ahead of you in traffic or at the market. Do a good deed; you may discover a renewed sense of your first love.

5. Overcoming - Fear

> Fear none of those things which thou shalt suffer: behold,
> the devil shall cast some of you into prison, that ye may be
> tried; and ye shall have tribulation ten days: be thou faith-
> ful unto death, and I will give thee a crown of life.
>
> Rev 2:10

CONTEXT

> *And unto the angel of the church in Smyrna write; These
> things saith the first and the last, which was dead, and is
> alive; I know thy works, and tribulation, and poverty, (but
> thou art rich) and I know the blasphemy of them which say
> they are Jews, and are not, but are the synagogue of Satan.*
> ***Fear none of those things which thou shalt suffer: be-
> hold, the devil shall cast some of you into prison, that ye
> may be tried; and ye shall have tribulation ten days: be
> thou faithful unto death, and I will give thee a crown of
> life.*** *He that hath an ear, let him hear what the Spirit saith
> unto the churches; He that overcometh shall not be hurt of
> the second death.*
>
> *Rev 2:8-11*

Oh how great is our salvation. The eternal God entered death
and is alive so that I may live in his eternity. My redemption grows
in value as I recognize the horror of my sin that caused God to
choose death in my place. My sorrow turns to celebration as I
enter into his resurrection. He was dead and is alive eternally. His
life is my new life, eternally. What a difference life makes when
viewed from an eternal perspective.

Eternity wanes when my treasure is found in wealth, power,
security and other things which will surely become of no value in
eternity. Jesus knows my condition. He looks at my brokenness
and calls me rich. He fills me with his Holy Spirit, and his richness
enables me to bear the poverty of this world and of my own life.

He knows the future I face. He knows of my trials, my failures and my unfaithfulness. He loves me, even knowing me. I am forgiven and I am given his power to overcome whatever comes my way, even my own failures.

His love casts out fear and his grace enables me to endure fearful things. A view of eternity always puts my problems in perspective. The crown of life awaits me in eternity but can become my countenance even today. Someday I will cast even that crown at his feet as I see the reality of his glory and the hopelessness of my condition. True life, eternal life, his life, will become a reality, and the joy of my salvation will be fulfilled in his richness.

The sting of sin, a second death, is not my future. My life is hid in Christ, eternally. Oh how great is his salvation!

Dear Lord Jesus:

You are faithful and any faithful part of me is from you. Thank you for the words "fear not." Even going through hard things need not be a "fear." You are with me and I can choose faithfulness. To me faith is relying on what you have said in your Word and the evidence of all that you have done in my life. It shows your love and gives me hope. It is one of the three things that remain. Problems come and go, only to be replaced by another. Yet, through it all you are faithful. Praise you Lord for life. It may be a crown someday, but it is life today.

Living in faith.

REFLECTION

Fear not what you suffer—it sounds like advice for life. *Be faithful until death*—it sounds like advice for the next life. Perhaps they are both for this life. In a little book called *Tuesdays with Morrie*, by Mitch Albom, a dying man says accepting or facing death makes life rich. Jesus says we are not of this world. A song says the things of earth grow strangely dim. How temporary this life is. It seems it would be easy to be faithful in view of life eternal, but it is hard. The flesh is a powerful force and yet it is death. Perhaps the "crown of life" is for this life. Perhaps it is valuing life in perspective of death and eternity. Then we, and I, can live fully, valuing my Lord and what is truly life.

PRACTICE

Just what does a crown of life look like? Is it a helmet to wear as protection from the pain of life? Is it a golden point of pride? Is it for public display or is it to be hidden away? Why would I even want one if the cost is tribulation?

Jesus wants me to have a crown of life and expects faithfulness to be its evidence. If Jesus wants to give it, it's good and worth any hardship I may endure in the process. Actually, I will endure hardship in this life. There is no escaping the trials of this world. The difference is, his grace is sufficient for any hardship.

I read the stories of those who have endured terrible pain or tragic loss and I say, "I could never handle that." The truth is, I could, not on my own, but in God's strength and through his grace. The truth is, whatever comes my way will be okay if I respond to his grace.

Problems carry with them seeds of bitterness and resentment. If I let these things dwell in my heart, resentment will kill my spirit and bitterness will poison the testimony of Christ in my life.

Problems also carry potential for faithfulness and overcoming. It is my choice, and strangely the crown of life begins to resemble a quality God calls humility. It is a crown which is not noticeable on the wearer. It is a transparent crown letting others see the grace of God in our lives and our attitude. It is redeeming and restoring to those who wear it.

Let nothing be done through strife or vainglory; but in lowliness of mind let each esteem other better than themselves. Look not every man on his own things, but every man also

on the things of others. Let this mind be in you, which was
also in Christ Jesus: Phil 2:3-5

It takes practice to wear a crown of life. Humility does not come naturally. It is a godly state, but one we can practice. The best way to grow in humility is to esteem others. A common precept is to not say anything if you can't say something good about someone. Practicing humility is not being quiet, saying nothing. Humility can be practiced by speaking positively to someone every day—the command is to esteem one another. To esteem we must become familiar with them, we must open ourselves to the risk of rejection. Esteeming requires noticing someone else in their own right, not in mine. Esteeming another will grow humility, and a transparent crown of life will reflect the grace of our Savior. What greater crown could life embody.

Practice humility, esteem someone today. Sneak up on them with words of kindness and affirmation. Don't let them deny the truth of God's love in themselves with false humility. We honor God when we recognize his hand of grace in the lives of others.

---

6. Overcoming - Sin

Repent; or else I will come unto thee quickly, and will fight against them with the sword of my mouth. Rev 2:16

CONTEXT

*And to the angel of the church in Pergamos write; These things saith he which hath the sharp sword with two edges; I know thy works, and where thou dwellest, even where Satan's seat is: and thou holdest fast my name, and hast not denied my faith, even in those days wherein Antipas was my faithful martyr, who was slain among you, where Satan dwelleth. But I have a few things against thee, because thou hast there them that hold the doctrine of Balaam, who taught Balac to cast a stumblingblock before the children of Israel, to eat things sacrificed unto idols, and to commit fornication. So hast thou also them that hold the doctrine of the Nicolaitans, which thing I hate. **Repent; or else I will come unto thee quickly, and will fight against them with the sword of my mouth.** He that hath an ear, let him hear what the Spirit saith unto the churches; To him that overcometh will I give to eat of the hidden manna, and will give him a white stone, and in the stone a new name written, which no man knoweth saving he that receiveth it.*   *Rev 2:12-17*

Talk about big trouble, Jesus has a sharp sword with two edges! Sometimes I think we all need a vision of our Savior in the dramatic form John saw him. Just considering such a vision of Christ would teach us the fear of God and hopefully turn us to true repentance. The Word of God is described in Scripture as a sword with two edges. It is a sword powerful enough to cut through our flesh and reveal spiritual truth.

For the word of God is quick, and powerful, and sharper than any twoedged sword, piercing even to the dividing asunder of soul and spirit, and of the joints and marrow, and is a discerner of the thoughts and intents of the heart.

Heb 4:12

The Word separates spirit and soul which are completely different in nature. When spiritual faith and soulish doctrine intermix, there is a contradiction that Jesus hates. However it is hidden, disguised or covered up, Jesus knows! He knows our faith and our works. He knows our circumstances and our heart.

Appreciating the truth that Jesus knows all is in itself both fearful and freeing. Where shall I hide my sin? I can't—I might as well repent. How can I handle impossible circumstances? I can't, but he can—I might as well rest in his strength.

As fearful as a vision of Jesus may be, its essence is he loves me. His sword is designed to draw us to repentance. Repentance is shown as a congregational issue in this letter; but it is also a national, community and an individual issue. Repent! The other option is a battle which cannot be won.

Repenting leads to overcoming, not in our self but in the strength of the Holy Spirit. It is a mystery, especially to those who do not understand spiritual things. Jesus taught in parables because people could not relate to spiritual truth (Matthew 13:13). Our life is also a mystery, one hidden in Christ but one waiting to be revealed in eternity.

Dear Lord Jesus:

Lord, why do we so often see spiritism and humanism in the church when they are so contradictory? The contradiction is expected in the world, but it still remains even from the early church. Today humanists see the new age as something spiritual, but deny you, Lord. It is truly something to repent of. I know that I would not want to fight against you, Lord. Teach me to repent quickly, Lord. Then I can rest in your peace and not struggle against you.

Praise you for fighting with the sword of your mouth, which I see as the truth—your Word. Truth is the sword against the lie of humanism and the deception of spiritism.

Repenting.

REFLECTION

"Repent or else;" these are strong words, especially for a church. Unbelievers need to believe, believers need to repent. It is almost easier to be an unbeliever. The psalmist wonders why the wicked prosper but sees their end as disaster (Psalm 73). I believe—no, I know—truth has a way of blessing; and one blessing is repentance, as hard as that may be. Jesus tells me what is wrong and leads me to repentance. I had to take the step of believing and I have to take the walk of repentance. It is an uphill walk but the view toward the top is worth it all, eternally.

PRACTICE

Repentance is not easy. It requires an acknowledgment of my sinful nature and a strong desire to change. We are not without help in the process. The Holy Spirit will search our ways and draw us to repentance, if we let him. Like the first step on a long journey, the hardest part is getting started. Repentance really is a process, one of continually being conformed to the image in which God originally created us—his own.

James describes the process of error as a downward cycle of choosing to defer the call to repentance. The choice becomes neglect and leads ultimately to death.

> *Let no man say when he is tempted, I am tempted of God: for God cannot be tempted with evil, neither tempteth he any man: But every man is tempted, when he is drawn away of his own lust, and enticed. Then when lust hath con-*

ceived, it bringeth forth sin: and sin, when it is finished, bringeth forth death. Do not err, my beloved brethren.

James 1:13-16

The process of repentance is the reverse. First, we must acknowledge sin and learn to hate its essence and consequence. Secondly, we must treasure the redemption which God has provided through his only Son, our Savior, Jesus Christ. Hating sin and valuing redemption will lead naturally to repentance. But repentance only brings us back to the beginning. Somehow we must get past continually repeating the cycle of temptation and repentance. The cycle ultimately destroyed biblical Israel; and the risk is just as real in our lives today.

But the first step is to learn to hate sin.

To practice hating sin, turn on the evening news and after every report of pain, violence or suffering, say out loud-sin caused that. Make it a habit to recognize the work of sin in every horrible event whether inflicted by man or nature. Soon sin will become so appalling the cycle can be broken.

---

7. Overcoming - Worldliness

But that which ye have already hold fast till I come.

Rev 2:25

CONTEXT

And unto the angel of the church in Thyatira write; These things saith the Son of God, who hath his eyes like unto a flame of fire, and his feet are like fine brass; I know thy works, and charity, and service, and faith, and thy patience, and thy works; and the last to be more than the first. Notwithstanding I have a few things against thee, because thou sufferest that woman Jezebel, which calleth herself a prophetess, to teach and to seduce my servants to commit fornication, and to eat things sacrificed unto idols. And I gave her space to repent of her fornication; and she repented not. Behold, I will cast her into a bed, and them that commit adultery with her into great tribulation, except they repent of their deeds. And I will kill her children with death; and all the churches shall know that I am he which searcheth the reins and hearts: and I will give unto every one of you according to your works. But unto you I say, and unto the rest in Thyatira, as many as have not this doctrine, and which have not known the depths of Satan, as they speak; I will put upon you none other burden. **But that which ye have already hold fast till I come.** *And he that overcometh, and keepeth my works unto the end, to him will I give power over the nations: And he shall rule them with a rod of iron; as the vessels of a potter shall they be broken to shivers: even as I received of my Father. And I will give him the morning star. He that hath an ear, let him hear what the Spirit saith unto the churches.*

Rev 2:18-29

Jesus is the Son of God. There is probably no greater way to describe him. I can picture flaming eyes and feet like fine brass; but to consider the Son of God requires entering into the depth of his character, the character of God himself.

It is a joy to also know the Son of God knows me and his body on this earth. How strengthening it is to know he can recognize the fruit of the Holy Spirit in me. He can see my love, my patience and my faith and recognize it as his own. It is his love, faith and patience that results in good works; works that serve the body of Christ and in so doing serve him. How comforting it is to hear that we are growing in the Lord. Growth is a slow process; and we often don't appreciate just how much the Holy Spirit is building our lives toward godliness.

The hope and promise of good to believers is a great contrast to the horror of judgment on those who lead others astray, especially the children of God.

> *It were better for him that a millstone were hanged about his neck, and he cast into the sea, than that he should offend one of these little ones.*　　　*Luke 17:1-2*

God gives time for repentance, but judgment is as sure as his Word. The depths of Satan are a deception and a snare. Better we should seek the deep things of our God, the one who has saved us and can keep us until the day of Jesus Christ. This is what we have and to which we can hold fast. It is Christ who is our rock and place of security. The prize is the morning star, Christ himself.

Dear Lord Jesus:

Patience is a virtue Lord, but it is not apathy. Godly patience is standing firm in hope. Holding fast takes strength. It takes being established and settled in faith. You search the "reins and the heart," Lord. You know my will and my desire, and you know they are often a contradiction. Line me up, Lord. Make me consistent in works, in ways and in my will. Praise you, Lord, for judging my failures, my sins and my wicked ways. Keep my fallenness under judgment until you come. Come quickly Lord, but as you tarry help me to hold fast. I am holding on to you, the rock of my salvation.

Hanging on.

REFLECTION

What do I have already? I have the wonderful gift of salvation. I have the wonderful gift of the Holy Spirit. I have the wonderful gift of his Word. I have faith, hope and love. I have the evidence of his presence in prayer and in the body of Christ. Wow! I sure have a lot. I have his chastening and correction. I have someone to cast my cares on and to be my strength in times of struggle. I have someone who loves me with his love. It is like a journal of gratefulness, and yet it is beyond that. It is something I can stand on and hold on to, but also release to bless others.

PRACTICE

The world would have me believe that every thing is relative. Mr. Einstein may have been right about the relativity of the physical universe but he also recognized the security in its laws and consistent truth. Truth is not relative; it is truth. It is something that is unshakeable and reliable, something to hold on to.

The depths of Satan may very well be his desire to make truth insecure. His opening words were "hath God said." What difference does faith, charity, patience and other steadfast attributes make in a world of relative values? The depths of Satan are horribly depressing; it is sin and its consequence—death.

But God said we can know the truth and it will free us from the bondage of relative worldliness. We have the assurance of his truth in his Word. We have the assurance of his presence in his Holy Spirit. We have the promise of his coming and the assurance of his overcoming power in our own spirit. We have a great gift and can

43

hold on to its truth.   There is nothing that can rob us of this precious promise.

> *For I am persuaded, that neither death, nor life, nor angels, nor principalities, nor powers, nor things present, nor things to come, Nor height, nor depth, nor any other creature, shall be able to separate us from the love of God, which is in Christ Jesus our Lord.*   Rom 8:38-39

The obvious way to practice holding on is to know what you have in Christ. The most practical expression of this advice is a journal of gratefulness. There is great benefit in counting your blessings and a permanence that is established by writing them down. The only problem is, it may take a lot of paper, for we have much to be grateful. Write it down and hold on. It is exciting!

---

8. Overcoming - Dead Works

> He that overcometh, the same shall be clothed in white raiment; and I will not blot out his name out of the book of life, but I will confess his name before my Father, and before his angels.
>
> Rev 3:5

CONTEXT

> *And unto the angel of the church in Sardis write; These things saith he that hath the seven Spirits of God, and the seven stars; I know thy works, that thou hast a name that thou livest, and art dead. Be watchful, and strengthen the things which remain, that are ready to die: for I have not found thy works perfect before God. Remember therefore how thou hast received and heard, and hold fast, and repent. If therefore thou shalt not watch, I will come on thee as a thief, and thou shalt not know what hour I will come upon thee. Thou hast a few names even in Sardis which have not defiled their garments; and they shall walk with me in white: for they are worthy.* **He that overcometh, the same shall be clothed in white raiment; and I will not blot out his name out of the book of life, but I will confess his name before my Father, and before his angels.** *He that hath an ear, let him hear what the Spirit saith unto the churches.*
>
> *Rev 3:1-6*

It is a freeing matter to realize the church belongs to Jesus Christ. It is he who holds the spirit and leadership of the church. He knows the works of the church and judges its vitality. We, of his church, bear his name and proclaim Jesus as Lord in life and in relationships. Then we proceed in our own ways and to do our own works—dead works. Martin Luther prayed about his ministry, knowing the risk of dead works:

"Use me as thy instrument in thy service. Only do not forsake me, for if I am left to myself, I will certainly bring it all to destruction. Amen"

Jesus says watch; wake up to life in the spirit, recognize that works without his spiritual life is dead. Jesus asked the disciples to watch and pray with him in the garden. They could not; and he was left alone to suffer the intensity of his calling, to die for our sins. Now he says to the church, watch and strengthen what remains which also is about to die. It is so easy to become discouraged in good works, even in ministry. Watch, remember what God has called us to and strengthen the remnant before it dies. Revival, renewal and restoration seem to be rooted in repentance and in standing on what we know is truth, even if it is just a remnant.

Without repentance the church becomes religious, which Karl Marx may rightly call an opiate. It is something that Jesus will destroy; and we will wonder why; after all, religion does things in Jesus name. His response could be, "I never knew you" (Matthew 7:22,23). Better we should enter into his judgement with repentance. Mercy will be found in the midst of judgement. Then restoration will come to the church and in individual lives. We will then abound in his grace.

We can be called overcomers, those of whom Jesus will say, "Come, ye blessed of my Father, inherit the kingdom prepared for you from the foundation of the world" (Matt 25:34).

Dear Lord Jesus:

Your words are strong, Lord. You can write and you can blot out. Is it a matter of repentance? Thank you, Lord, for coming unto me quickly and bringing me to the point of repentance. In my flesh is no good thing and all I deserve is blotting out, but you love me with your love and bring me to repentance. Praise you, Lord, for loving me with your love; I look forward to white rainment. Even more so I look forward to your presence. Help me to see it and to live it; keep me repentant.

Repenting.

REFLECTION

There is something for me to do—it's to overcome. There are many things to overcome: the world, the flesh and the devil. They are all death, but I have life and have it abundantly. The world is bound in foolishness, my flesh is bent on dying and my enemy is purposed for destruction. They are all vain, but all are highly verbal and even deceptively believable. I am in another kingdom, a kingdom of heaven (not of this world), of spirit (not of the flesh), and of God (not of the devil). My Lord has overcome these and I can also, in his power, in his Word and in his Spirit. I do have to choose and watch. I do have to pray and trust. I do have to obey.

PRACTICE

Therefore leaving the principles of the doctrine of Christ, let us go on unto perfection; not laying again the foundation of repentance from dead works, and of faith toward God,
Heb 6:1

The Bible considers repentance from dead works to be a foundational principal. It is something that is a beginning point and not something we should continually struggle with. The author of Hebrews was frustrated because Christians seem to continually struggle with basics. It isn't much different today. I have struggled for years with common failures and wonder why I don't make great spiritual progress. The problem may be that my repentance is incomplete. Paul speaks of godly sorrow that leads to repentance and clearing of our souls (2 Corinthians 7:9-11). Godly sorrow, I think, is recognizing the sorrow that our Lord has when he gave himself for our sin.

Repentance begins with hating sin. In the exercise on hating sin we practiced recognizing the horrible works of sin by seeing horrible violence and tragedy as the result of sin. Now we can take another step and that is to value our redemption. To know the pain of our Savior as he bore my sin. He didn't generally bear the sins of the world; he bore my sin, all of it. Just an inkling of that pain brings godly sorrow into my heart. I can see and regret the consequences of my sin in the world and in my life. There is healing for that pain. There is no other healing for the pain my sin caused Christ. Only repentance heals so his love can begin the work of restoration in my life.

Turn on the evening news again. After every act and incidence of tragedy say, "sin caused that," then say, "it caused my savior to suffer and die." Hatred of sin will grow into godly sorrow. Hating sin and valuing redemption not only leads to repentance, it builds a carefulness and a zeal in us that "lets us go on unto perfection" in Christ.

9. Overcoming - Aloneness

I know thy works: behold, I have set before thee an open door, and no man can shut it: for thou hast a little strength, and hast kept my word, and hast not denied my name.

Rev 3:8

CONTEXT

And to the angel of the church in Philadelphia write; These things saith he that is holy, he that is true, he that hath the key of David, he that openeth, and no man shutteth; and shutteth, and no man openeth; **I know thy works: behold, I have set before thee an open door, and no man can shut it: for thou hast a little strength, and hast kept my word, and hast not denied my name.** *Behold, I will make them of the synagogue of Satan, which say they are Jews, and are not, but do lie; behold, I will make them to come and worship before thy feet, and to know that I have loved thee. Because thou hast kept the word of my patience, I also will keep thee from the hour of temptation, which shall come upon all the world, to try them that dwell upon the earth. Behold, I come quickly: hold that fast which thou hast, that no man take thy crown. Him that overcometh will I make a pillar in the temple of my God, and he shall go no more out: and I will write upon him the name of my God, and the name of the city of my God, which is new Jerusalem, which cometh down out of heaven from my God: and I will write upon him my new name. He that hath an ear, let him hear what the Spirit saith unto the churches.*

Rev 3:7-13

Philadelphia, the city of brotherly love—its meaning may very well reflect its character. It's the only letter in which the church is commended without exception. I have visited the modern namesake of this biblical city and love the heritage of liberty it expresses. I found caring, loving people but know also of depravity and sin that lives there. Those of the synagogue of Satan are alive and well today, even in the place of brotherly love—the church. Regardless, he who is holy and true commends our strength and our fidelity to his name, his character, and the expression of his love to one another. It is the name of a city, a church and a life proclaiming we are not alone.

He is holy and true; he also has the key of David. Sometimes it is easier to see God as a spirit, holy and true; then we don't have to deal with the implications of kingdom living. We are called, as a body and as individuals, to keep the word of his patience. Patience is a lot harder when others are involved, but the blessings are well worth it. Impatience has allowed the power of temptation to enter my life on more than one occasion. How much better it is to hold fast to that which we have. It takes a little strength—the strength he gives us to be faithful to his name.

The fact that we have a little strength implies it will be tested. It is likely to be tested in relationship. It is likely to be tested in our commitment to love one another with the love with which God loves us. If we overcome, if we love with patience, our city of brotherly love will get a new name. It will be the city of God, who is love.

The open door to choose and express love is set before us every day. We can choose to enter in. It is a choice, a continual choice, one that is at odds with the world but in harmony with the *kingdom of God's dear Son* (Col 1:13).

Dear Lord Jesus:

You do indeed know my works, both good and wicked. You chasten me in my error and guide me in my truth. If I have any strength, it is yours. It is the strength you promised to build in me as you settle and establish me (1 Peter 5:10). I can have strength to overcome, be settled in your Word and established in your name.

50

Praise to you, Lord, for an open door to your kingdom. Let it reflect itself as an open door in my life. Help me to communicate your truth, Lord, in a way that is true and in a way that builds your life in the church and in individuals.

Holding fast.

REFLECTION

The sermon topic at church recently was focused on "Entering Into His Promise." The Lord has promised good to me and for my family. I want to enter into his goodness; it is an open door. Life is like a hallway; there are many doors and most are closed. I seem to want to enter the closed doors—it's the way of my flesh. My Lord has set an open door before me. It is not just open; it's before me. Why can't I see it? I need to pray for open eyes to see an open door. I need to pray for a little strength to enter the open door.

PRACTICE

In the garden of Eden, Adam had it all. He lived in paradise, exercised the power of dominion and enjoyed open fellowship with God. What could be better—but God had a concern.

> *And the LORD God said, It is not good that the man should be alone; I will make him an help meet for him. Gen 2:18*

We are created to be in relationship; and relationships are designed to express love. It is only in relationship that love can be both given and expressed. Isolation and aloneness are the work of our enemy. The roaring lion seeks to devour those who are isolated; and the greatest element of isolation is sin. The wages of sin are called death; and surely death is ultimate aloneness.

God had a better idea—he created us in relationship with himself and created others for relationship in every aspect of our life.

When we are born again in his spirit we are automatically in relationship with those of the same spirit—his Holy Spirit. We may choose not to walk in the fruit of the relationship, but it is a reality none the less. Relationships of heart, mind, soul and body are all designed to be true and holy. To isolate our self is to deny his name and his calling to godly relationships.

I know that my greatest failures in spirit and life have come when I entered the temptation of aloneness. Praise to God for his chastening in love—it turns us back to his fellowship and restores us to the richness of loving relationships in the body of Christ.

Flee aloneness, enter the open door, find and express caring relationships.

To practice redemptive relationships, use a lifeline—phone a friend today. Reach out, the door is open and before you. Choose life, choose love, choose to live in a caring relationship. It is the will of God for you.

---

10. Overcoming - Apathy

> ... and anoint thine eyes with eyesalve, that thou mayest see. As many as I love, I rebuke and chasten: be zealous therefore, and repent.   Rev 3:18b-19

CONTEXT

> *And unto the angel of the church of the Laodiceans write; These things saith the Amen, the faithful and true witness, the beginning of the creation of God; I know thy works, that thou art neither cold nor hot: I would thou wert cold or hot. So then because thou art lukewarm, and neither cold nor hot, I will spue thee out of my mouth. Because thou sayest, I am rich, and increased with goods, and have need of nothing; and knowest not that thou art wretched, and miserable, and poor, and blind, and naked: I counsel thee to buy of me gold tried in the fire, that thou mayest be rich; and white raiment, that thou mayest be clothed, and that the shame of thy nakedness do not appear; **and anoint thine eyes with eyesalve, that thou mayest see. As many as I love, I rebuke and chasten: be zealous therefore, and repent.** Behold, I stand at the door, and knock: if any man hear my voice, and open the door, I will come in to him, and will sup with him, and he with me. To him that overcometh will I grant to sit with me in my throne, even as I also overcame, and am set down with my Father in his throne. He that hath an ear, let him hear what the Spirit saith unto the churches.*   *Rev 3:14-22*

Jesus calls himself the Amen, the faithful and true witness, and the beginning of creation. He affirms that he is the essence of all things. Creation began with him and will conclude being fulfilled in him. The process of time and our very lives are upheld in the truth and faithfulness of Christ.

Ho-hum, life goes on. We have bills to pay, children to care for and a frantic life to support. I have heard it said that the opposite of love is not hate, but apathy. How true it is. Of all the churches addressed in these letters, this one is without commendation. Nothing to be said for it—apathy kills it. Jesus says it would be better if they were hot or cold. The love of God draws those who are hot toward himself. The fear of God can turn those who are cold toward him. The lukewarm are insensitive to love and fear—apathy that steals the essence of life. Apathy, a picture of the insensitivity of death itself.

Apathy is called wretched, miserable, poor, blind and naked—who cares. Actually blindness causes apathy to consider itself rich and meaningful. What arrogance, what deception. Apathy is blind not being able to see its true state or even its danger. Apathy thinks it sees but its very light is darkness. Apathy cannot see death though it stands at the very brink. It cannot see eternity though it faces it every day. What wretched darkness apathy works.

Jesus stands at the door and knocks. He is an open door, but ours can be closed and locked by apathy. Still he knocks, still he loves us—even while we are born sinners. His knock may come in the form of chastisement, but it is love. He is not apathetic; he cares, he initiates our ability to hear and to have our own poverty revealed so we can repent. The excitement of zeal can be restored in our lives as he sups with us. A sense of his presence will keep us from apathy and fill us with zeal.

Dear Lord Jesus:

Help me to see, Lord. Help me to hear, Lord. I open the door; come in and sup with me. Thank you that your rebuke and chastening are proof of your love for me. Zeal is a quality I desire. Repentance is a choice I make. Build my zeal for you and your Word. Lord, that gives my life spirit. Chasten and rebuke me, Lord. Give me eyes to see so that I can repent. I want to see clearly, Lord. I want to see your open door, and I want to open my door to your desire. Teach me, show me, sup with me and I with you.

Zealous.

REFLECTION

Zeal is a wonderful word to my Lord. I see it in his character. He is zealous for the Father's glory. He is zealous for the hurting and for those who are lost. He is even zealous against the wicked and evil. His zeal was perfected in his suffering, his death and in his resurrection. It was the zeal of his love for me. What is love without zeal? Even a quiet love is filled with emotion and caring. My Lord's zeal was not quiet; it turned the world upside down. It still does. He is zealous for me. I can be zealous for him in both quiet and active ways.

PRACTICE

The apostle Paul was a picture of zeal. He was as zealous against the church as he was for the gospel, after his conversion. His own testimony is reflected in his letters, specifically:

> *Concerning zeal, persecuting the church; touching the righteousness which is in the law, blameless. But what things were gain to me, those I counted loss for Christ.*
>
> *Phil 3:6-7*

It may not be necessary to be knocked off of a horse, or to have a mystical experience with God, to turn our zeal. Much of the process is left in our own hands. Jesus says anoint our eyes with eye-salve so that we may see our true state. Then we are to buy what is precious from him, true riches and righteousness.

What is the currency of Christ? How do I buy the treasure of his glory and the covering of his righteousness? Isaiah says to the thirsty: "come ye to the waters, and he that hath no money; come ye, buy, and eat; yea, come, buy wine and milk without money and without price" (Isa 55:1,3). He concludes the passage with words from God: "Incline your ear, and come unto me: hear, and your soul shall live; and I will make an everlasting covenant with you, even the sure mercies of David."

His currency is the currency of hearing. His price is a price we cannot pay. Open the door, let his presence show the depravity of our poverty so that the price he has already paid can be received. Then zeal will lead us to repentance and then to obedience.

Practice hearing, practice repentance, do it with zeal. Begin with repentance of apathy. The exercise is a hard one, it means sacrifice without recognition. Today, give something of value away in a way that you cannot be recognized. Give a hundred dollars, or an amount significant to you, to a need that you see. The important step is not the giving, it is the seeing. Apathy will flee from the light of caring that results in action.

---

11. Worship in Humility

The four and twenty elders fall down before him that sat on the throne, and worship him that liveth for ever and ever, and cast their crowns before the throne, saying,

Rev 4:10

CONTEXT

After this I looked, and, behold, a door was opened in heaven: and the first voice which I heard was as it were of a trumpet talking with me; which said, Come up hither, and I will shew thee things which must be hereafter. And immediately I was in the spirit: and, behold, a throne was set in heaven, and one sat on the throne. And he that sat was to look upon like a jasper and a sardine stone: and there was a rainbow round about the throne, in sight like unto an emerald. And round about the throne were four and twenty seats: and upon the seats I saw four and twenty elders sitting, clothed in white raiment; and they had on their heads crowns of gold. And out of the throne proceeded lightnings and thunderings and voices: and there were seven lamps of fire burning before the throne, which are the seven Spirits of God. And before the throne there was a sea of glass like unto crystal: and in the midst of the throne, and round about the throne, were four beasts full of eyes before and behind. And the first beast was like a lion, and the second beast like a calf, and the third beast had a face as a man, and the fourth beast was like a flying eagle. And the four beasts had each of them six wings about him; and they were full of eyes within: and they rest not day and night, saying, Holy, holy, holy, Lord God Almighty, which was, and is, and is to come. And when those beasts give glory and honour and thanks to him that sat on the throne, who liveth for ever and ever, **The four and**

twenty elders fall down before him that sat on the throne,
and worship him that liveth for ever and ever, and cast
their crowns before the throne, saying, Thou art worthy,
O Lord, to receive glory and honour and power: for thou
hast created all things, and for thy pleasure they are and
were created.   *Rev 4:1-11*

A common perception of heaven is as a quiet place, where we play a harp sitting on a cloud somewhere. The reality of heaven is that it is a noisy, busy place. There are elders, beasts, spirits, angels—the host of God's creation. The most predominate feature of heaven is a throne, which also is not quiet. Heaven is a reality, and the business of heaven seems to be worship directed to the resident of the throne, the Lord God Almighty.

John saw this vision of heaven in the spirit, but it is not likely that it was just some mystical experience. Predominate among the teachings of Jesus was the kingdom of God and of heaven. Both John the Baptist and Jesus proclaimed the kingdom to be at hand (Matt 3:2, 4:17). Later the disciples were instructed to go and preach that same message (Matt 10:7).

The reality of heaven may be closer than we think. Dallas Willard in his classic book, *The Divine Conspiracy*, relates this proximity and availability as if one would say electricity is at hand. The power is there; all we have to do is believe it and use it. When we do, the response will be worship. When we do, worship will express praise but demonstrate humility. The beginning of worship is to cast our crowns before the throne. He alone is worthy. We are his creation. We only exist because of his love. We can worship only because of his grace.

Dear Lord Jesus:

You are the one who sits on the throne; King of glory, honor and power. Whatever crowns I have, including the crown of my life, is before you. My only response to holiness is worship. My only response to holiness is releasing all that I think I have. The truth is I have nothing except for you. The truth is you love me and lift me up to your kingdom. I don't even deserve to be in it, but you love me and made it possible for me to love you, to fear you and to honor you.

Praise to you.

REFLECTION

Falling down before him is to worship him. He is the King of all creation and we are the only part that has been redeemed. How much he must love me. How unworthy of that I am. How needy I am, not only of his salvation but of his presence. He is holy; I am unholy, but he makes me holy in himself. Praise to the King of Glory, my Lord and Savior. He is holy and I bow down in his presence. Holiness is like a vacuum; it draws me into itself and fills my life. Bowing down is a choice, a choice to worship, a choice to surrender to holiness.

PRACTICE

There are two things which we must know about heaven. First, its center is a throne and second, its sphere is worship. There is very little in heaven that does not recognize the glory of God on a throne and respond in worship. If the kingdom of heaven is to be at hand then we must find place for the Lord in the throne of our lives.

A popular evangelistic pamphlet called *The Four Spiritual Laws* depicts our life as an open throne. At issue is who will reside on the throne. We can occupy the throne in pride and self-centeredness. We can allow the enemy of our soul to occupy the throne in deception and sin. The decision we need to make and live out is to let the Lord reside in our throne by honoring his Word as a path of life.

The response of the elders in John's vision of heaven was to fall down, to worship and to cast their crowns before the throne. Scriptural worship is often misunderstood. We go to church and attend a worship service. Then we leave and wonder—what did I get out of it?

Worship in scripture has only one meaning. In both old and new testament, the word means to prostrate oneself. *Strong's Concordance* offers a definition indicating the root word means to kiss and includes an example of a dog licking its masters hand. Worship is humiliating; we have to give up our crowns, we have to bow down, we have to acknowledge our unworthiness.

> *O come, let us worship and bow down: let us kneel before*
> *the LORD our maker.*   *Ps 95:6*

Learn to practice worship. Initially it will be hard; regardless of how we claim to like humility, the truth is we resist it. Worship is too risky, we might lose ourselves in it. Try it; go into someplace safe. Don't just bow down, prostrate yourself and speak words of praise. Acknowledge your unworthiness and his worthiness. Experience true worship, it will make us ready for heaven at hand, and in eternity.

---

12. Worship in Song

And they sung a new song, saying, Thou art worthy to take the book, and to open the seals thereof: for thou wast slain, and hast redeemed us to God by thy blood out of every kindred, and tongue, and people, and nation;　Rev 5:9

CONTEXT

And I saw in the right hand of him that sat on the throne a book written within and on the backside, sealed with seven seals. And I saw a strong angel proclaiming with a loud voice, Who is worthy to open the book, and to loose the seals thereof? And no man in heaven, nor in earth, neither under the earth, was able to open the book, neither to look thereon. And I wept much, because no man was found worthy to open and to read the book, neither to look thereon. And one of the elders saith unto me, Weep not: behold, the Lion of the tribe of Juda, the Root of David, hath prevailed to open the book, and to loose the seven seals thereof. And I beheld, and, lo, in the midst of the throne and of the four beasts, and in the midst of the elders, stood a Lamb as it had been slain, having seven horns and seven eyes, which are the seven Spirits of God sent forth into all the earth. And he came and took the book out of the right hand of him that sat upon the throne. And when he had taken the book, the four beasts and four and twenty elders fell down before the Lamb, having every one of them harps, and golden vials full of odours, which are the prayers of saints. **And they sung a new song, saying, Thou art worthy to take the book, and to open the seals thereof: for thou wast slain, and hast redeemed us to God by thy blood out of every kindred, and tongue, and people, and nation;** *And hast made us unto our God kings and priests: and we shall reign on the earth.*　*Rev 5:1-10*

61

One assurance in Scripture is, God has a plan. He has a plan for our lives and a plan for his creation. The fullness of the plan itself may be a sealed mystery and even undiscoverable by man, but our Lord, the lion of Judah, root of David and lamb of God, is the one by which the great plan of God unfolds. Pilate called Jesus the King of the Jews and sentenced him as the slain lamb—both are a reality in eternity. The lion and the lamb are one in Christ.

John wept when he realized that no man could open the book. It is truly a sad condition to be without Christ. We are dead in our sin without Christ. The potential for our lives created in the image of God is lost without Christ. Truly there is great cause for weeping without Christ. The resolution is "Weep not: behold." God not only has a plan he has the means to implement it and the center of the plan is Jesus Christ. The lion of Judah and the lamb who was slain has the authority to open God's plan and in righteousness he will bring it to pass.

Jesus said that he was in the midst of those who were gathered in his name (Matt 18:20). He is in the midst of the throne and of those who are gathered around the throne. What comfort it is knowing the presence and centrality of Christ in our lives. It is no surprise that the response of the redeemed is to worship. There is a new song, it is the song of the redeemed. It is the song that will fill eternity with the amazing grace of God who gave his only Son for our redemption.

Dear Lord Jesus:

You alone are worthy to judge the world and to see your redemption completed. You have redeemed me by your blood. I am one out of every kindred; a stranger to the covenant, but you loved me. How great your love is for me—you redeemed me. Millions of angels praise you, but you want my praise. You don't need praise, although you are worthy. You desire my praise because you love me and want me to be fulfilled in my redemption.

Treasuring redemption.

REFLECTION

What have I to sing about except God's redemption; the song of the redeemed. Singing is a special gift that God has given man, created in his image. After all, God sings, *he will joy over us with singing* (Zeph 3:17). His song is the song of redemption, my song is the song of the redeemed. Praise to my savior who gives me something to sing about. Without redemption all my songs are the blues. The world sings a sad song, it's no wonder. I can sing with God, the song of the redeemed, a new song.

PRACTICE

Singing seems to be a natural expression of praise. In reality, it is a special gift and has a very special place in eternity. An interesting question to ask is, who sings? Scripture is filled with singing people. Mostly they are rejoicing in God's provision. Moses, Miriam and the children of Israel are the first really organized singers in Scripture. It was a song of praise for God's mighty deliverance. David is known for singing, and Psalms is a song book of praises.

Unfortunately, singing in itself is passive. When Moses came down from he mountain he heard singing in the camp; and it was not a song of praise to God. How sad the music of the world is. We can sing for joy, but the world sings the blues. Hopelessness inhabits the songs of the world regardless of genre.

Who sings: God sings, he is the redeemer, and creation sings, it shall be renewed. But conspicuously absent from Scripture's list of singers are angels. Regardless of popular concepts and Christmas music, angels just don't seem to sing. Angels speak, talk, command, charge, protest, call out, commune and otherwise express themselves verbally but apparently without music. Although they play a mean trumpet, angels may not sing because they are not redeemed. Could it be that God has given us something special, a gift of song to rejoice in our redemption. Angels are not redeemed and those who are fallen have no hope of redemption; what have they to sing about?

In heaven many are offering praise to God and to the Lamb. There are only three who do it with singing; the 24 elders (Rev 5:9), the redeemed (Rev 14:3) and the overcomers (Rev 15:3). These are all individuals who have experienced his redemption.

Speaking to yourselves in psalms and hymns and spiritual songs, singing and making melody in your heart to the Lord;
Eph 5:19

Practice rejoicing in redemption, sing a song to God. Rejoice in the words of *Amazing Grace*. It's a new song; it's the song of the redeemed.

13. Worship in Praise

And every creature which is in heaven, and on the earth, and under the earth, and such as are in the sea, and all that are in them, heard I saying, Blessing, and honour, and glory, and power, be unto him that sitteth upon the throne, and unto the Lamb for ever and ever.   Rev 5:13

CONTEXT

And I beheld, and I heard the voice of many angels round about the throne and the beasts and the elders: and the number of them was ten thousand times ten thousand, and thousands of thousands; Saying with a loud voice, Worthy is the Lamb that was slain to receive power, and riches, and wisdom, and strength, and honour, and glory, and blessing. **And every creature which is in heaven, and on the earth, and under the earth, and such as are in the sea, and all that are in them, heard I saying, Blessing, and honour, and glory, and power, be unto him that sitteth upon the throne, and unto the Lamb for ever and ever.** *And the four beasts said, Amen. And the four and twenty elders fell down and worshipped him that liveth for ever and ever.*   *Rev 5:11-14*

The song of redemption is sufficient to cause all of God's creation to praise the Lamb that was slain—our Lord and Savior, Jesus Christ. The only exception are those who have rejected his marvelous grace. The fallen angels and those who are subject to his wrath surely have no reason to praise, only to fear without hope.

> *But a certain fearful looking for of judgment and fiery indignation, which shall devour the adversaries.*
> *Heb 10:27*

The works of God in creation were mighty. With his word he brought into being all that exists. He created life and breathed it into a creature whom he made in his own image. If that were all God ever did, it would be sufficient to praise him forever. A song sung by children at Passover proclaims *Dayenu!*—it would have been enough. Each of God's steps in the miraculous deliverance of Israel from bondage is recited and followed with the children's chorus, Dayenu!

All of God's works are mighty and worthy of praise, but one work makes all the others pale in comparison. There is one work that is more than an expression of his power and might. There is one work that cost him his only Son. It was the work of love, a love so great that he gave his only Son so that whosoever believed would not perish, but have everlasting life (John 3:16). It is this work that the host of heaven praise—the Lamb that was slain. The beneficiaries of this work of love sing the song of the redeemed. The angels who have witnessed his great mercy and know the cost, praise the Lamb, the one who carried the pain of death and overcame.

It is the Lamb that was slain who sits on the throne, who holds the future in his hands. He is worthy to open the seals, releasing the wrath of God and the revenge of his beloved. It is the Lamb who was slain who holds my future. When I realize his suffering, the pain of my own sin, there is no other response for me but to worship and praise him.

Dear Lord Jesus:

All of the living creation praise God, but the elders worship. Praise you, Lord, for you are the lamb who is worthy. Worthy to receive all things: power, riches, wisdom, strength, honor, blessing and glory. It is a long list but you are indeed worthy, for you have overcome. You have redeemed your beloved, and you have established truth and salvation. All creation groans for the day, Lord; the day when all things will be made new. It is something for me to sing about and to fall down in worship. Then, in humility, will I find, and live in, the joy of your salvation

                                  Groaning in joy.

REFLECTION

The Psalms conclude exhorting every thing that has breath to praise the Lord (150:6). I have breath, I need to praise him. The rest of his breathing creation praises him by being what they are created to be. I alone have the potential for rebellion. Praise comes natural to the creatures; I must choose. It is strange to think of a creature praising God, but it does. It lives out its life fulfilling its created purpose. What greater praise is there than that? My created purpose is to live in his image, and I am fallen from that place. My praise may be vocal, but ultimately my life must be restored to a living praise. Creatures praise God by being themselves. I praise God by not being my fallen self.

PRACTICE

Praise is enlarging God. He is said to inhabit the praises of his people (Ps 22:3) and as we praise, his habitation is enlarged in us and in his creation. Praise is recognizing him by recounting his character and his ways. It is remembering his works and recounting his faithfulness in the past. Praise then moves from theology to practice. The purpose of praise is not just to say nice things about God, but to see our life change and the good news of his grace change the lives of others. It is an enlarging experience.

The effect of praise is that his character is worked into our lives. As our praise matures we become more like him in character and behavior. A popular quip today is "WWJD" or "What Would Jesus Do?" To live this saying requires knowing his character; and praise may be an effective path to appropriating both the knowledge and the expression of his ways.

In Scripture, all of creation gives praise to God. Even creatures and living things give him praise. Mountains are pictured praising him. Could it be that their praise is embodied in what they are? A lily is created to be beautiful and just doing so praises its creator. We, unfortunately, are fallen from the state of praising by just being. In our fallen state, just being dishonors our creator. What a horrible position sin has delivered us to. We are unable to fulfill our created purpose and praise the one who created us, by just being.

Our spiritual man chooses to praise God, but it is so easily quenched by our tendency toward the flesh and the world. We must choose to praise and let it be lived out in life.

Practice praise by giving God credit for the growth in your life. Reflect on a way God has changed you and tell someone about it. Praise will grow in you and be a seed for celebration in another.

14. Vision in God

And I saw when the Lamb opened one of the seals, and I heard, as it were the noise of thunder, one of the four beasts saying, Come and see.

Rev 6:1

CONTEXT

And I saw when the Lamb opened one of the seals, and I heard, as it were the noise of thunder, one of the four beasts saying, Come and see. And I saw, and behold a white horse: and he that sat on him had a bow; and a crown was given unto him: and he went forth conquering, and to conquer. And when he had opened the second seal, I heard the second beast say, Come and see. And there went out another horse that was red: and power was given to him that sat thereon to take peace from the earth, and that they should kill one another: and there was given unto him a great sword. And when he had opened the third seal, I heard the third beast say, Come and see. And I beheld, and lo a black horse; and he that sat on him had a pair of balances in his hand. And I heard a voice in the midst of the four beasts say, A measure of wheat for a penny, and three measures of barley for a penny; and see thou hurt not the oil and the wine. And when he had opened the fourth seal, I heard the voice of the fourth beast say, Come and see. And I looked, and behold a pale horse: and his name that sat on him was Death, and Hell followed with him. And power was given unto them over the fourth part of the earth, to kill with sword, and with hunger, and with death, and with the beasts of the earth. Rev 6:1-8

Come and see are the words John heard. They may be what the church is called to proclaim today. We can enter into the vision of God for salvation; and then our call is to go and preach the good news of the kingdom of heaven (Matt. 10:7). Come and see the glory of God. Come and see the grace, faithfulness, judgements and fear of God.

When the church says come and see, the implications are broad. Often we limit the vision in God to our pleasure—we want to see the love of God and his provision. God is much more. Come and see means to enter into his fulness, which includes the fear of God. Judgement preaching may not be popular today, but it is part of come and see. When we do openly come and see, the love of God and the fear of God will both draw us into the grace of God and his salvation in the Lord Jesus Christ.

When I choose Christ the conflict begins. Darkness and light are contrary, and the white horse will surely upset the seeming peace of my darkness. His arrows of the word of truth will pierce my soul and divide spirit from flesh. His crown will test my faithfulness and examine the words I utter when I sing *Trust and Obey*. He conquers and will conquer. In him I am victorious. I may witness war, famine and pestilence. They may even take my life; but they can never take my eternal life. The kingdom of heaven is truly at hand.

The horses of war, famine and pestilence are as prevalent today as ever. Men who are commanded to love one another devise ways of destroying each other. The earth which is created to nourish man is abused until it is devoid of resources. Disease does not seem to have an end. Plague destroyed a third of the population, largely because of man's refuse. Today aids threatens to do the same, because of man's lust. Pogo was right—we are our own enemy.

Dear Lord Jesus:

Four seals of God with four beasts, each saying come and see. Conflict, war, famine and death were opened and all of these are evident in the world today. Praise to you, Lord, for life and also for your Holy Spirit which lets us come and see. I can see your hand of grace and judgement in the world and also in my life. What I see is your glory. You are able to open the seals. You are also able to save and to bless and keep. You are able to judge. All of it is praiseworthy for you are not only able you are worthy. I can see you even in the midst of spiritual conflict, and the judgment of war, famine and death. It is my salvation.

Seeing

REFLECTION

John heard "as it were the noise of thunder." I hear a still small voice, one that is easy to ignore. How can I get the voice of the Holy Spirit to be louder? Is it to listen more, pray more, obey more, or what? Perhaps it is all of these things. Ascetics seek vision in God—some find peace, others turmoil. I think I am who I am and need to listen as much as anything. I need to ask and then expect to hear. Too often I ask and then go on with life. God speaks, but the noise of the world prevails. I know he told me he loves me with his love. Do I need more? Yes, I need him daily because life is daily.

PRACTICE

To have a vision in God is really just to see things from his perspective. Many of us want to have a vision of God, but are not prepared to respond like Isaiah:

> *Then said I, Woe is me! for I am undone; because I am a man of unclean lips, and I dwell in the midst of a people of unclean lips: for mine eyes have seen the King, the LORD of hosts."*   Isa 6:5

A vision of God would be terrifying and most likely portend some difficult ministry. Most of us, especially myself, do not really seek a vision of God. What we can and should seek is vision *in* God. Scripture is designed for us to see things from God's perspective, especially our salvation. To see myself as a sinner is

God's viewpoint. To see him as Savior is also his viewpoint. To enter his salvation is to have a vision in God and to respond in obedience.

I have heard it said that the holocaust was God's will. My conscience rebels at such an idea, it is too horrible to even consider. However, from God's perspective, what would it take for men to have the zeal to establish a nation of Israel? What persecution would drive men from their homes and ignite the fervor to fight and die for a new nation? It's the heritage of America and has become the heritage of Israel. Persecution may not be God's will, but it surely shows his working of all things, even the horrors of sin, to the good of those who love him (Romans 8:28).

> Practice seeing a vision in God. Find the good that he works in your life when something seemingly bad happens. It is a grand view from his point—it may give you the endurance needed to overcome in the circumstance.

15. Waiting on God

And white robes were given unto every one of them; and it was said unto them, that they should rest yet for a little season, until their fellowservants also and their brethren, that should be killed as they were, should be fulfilled.

Rev 6:11

CONTEXT

And when he had opened the fifth seal, I saw under the altar the souls of them that were slain for the word of God, and for the testimony which they held: And they cried with a loud voice, saying, How long, O Lord, holy and true, dost thou not judge and avenge our blood on them that dwell on the earth? **And white robes were given unto every one of them; and it was said unto them, that they should rest yet for a little season, until their fellowservants also and their brethren, that should be killed as they were, should be fulfilled.** *Rev 6:9-11*

There is no one to say come and see when the fifth seal is opened. No explanation is necessary. Those who have died violently for the word and testimony of God are under the altar, at the very foot of Jesus Christ in glory. The blood of martyrs cries out on earth as we read their testimony and hear of persecution and death in current events. All of their voices cry out in heaven. Their cry is for the vengeance of God. Vengeance is still the Lord's, even in eternity. The blessing of this sight is that the martyrs are alive. They are a living testimony of the psalmist's words:

The LORD is on my side; I will not fear: what can man do unto me? *Ps 118:6*

73

What is God waiting on? Why do the wicked seem to prosper? Where is my healing, my deliverance, my desire? God says wait. In the meantime we learn to be clothed in his righteousness. The robes of his purity. Wait! It is likely to be one of the most difficult answers we face. All of our culture says rush, do it now, go for it. God says wait. The reason for God's delay is real; it is a quality of his character—his longsuffering. He knows the fulness of times.

Even with the word wait, God has a blessing for us: rest. Rest for a season, even in the trials of living.

> *But the God of all grace, who hath called us unto his eternal glory by Christ Jesus, after that ye have suffered a while, make you perfect, stablish, strengthen, settle you.*
>
> *1 Pet 5:10*

Dear Lord Jesus:

Sometimes I cry out "How long, O Lord." My impatience is trivial compared to the souls of the martyrs. Even heaven is impatient for your return, but you have perfect timing. I cry out "How long" over little things, but looking back I can see how I grew during the time. Teach me to be content to live in this day, not being anxious for tomorrow or dwelling on the past. Today is your day for me. I live in today with faith from yesterday and hope for tomorrow. Your day will come, Lord. In the meantime I will rest with the souls who love you and are called to your purpose.

Resting in you

REFLECTION

It does not seem like life is a waiting time. There is always something in process. The secret is to rest in it. I need to learn to live not from event to event, but to just live life. Even in prayer it is easy to pray through one set of circumstance only to face another

74

need. There will always be events or needs until restoration is complete. My prayer needs to focus on Jesus and on praise for who he is and what he has done. Events and circumstances will resolve themselves, some positively and some negatively, but life is eternal. I can live eternally now, it is called rest. Rest is not inactivity; in fact it may even be busier. Rest is living without anxiety and in hope.

PRACTICE

Stop The World I Want To Get Off! It was a popular motion picture from the post-war fifties that laughed at our increasing tension and hurried state. It is no laughing matter today. Stress related illnesses prevail, and the lives of individuals and families are fractured into a frenzy of activity. I saw an advertisement recently that pictured a man relaxing on the beach with his laptop computer. One thing that ad would never do is sell me a computer; the beach and rest are an antithesis of work. If the laptop and cell phone become appendages to life, then stay away from the beach: salt air and sand are not good for them. Back from the beach, cell phones and other means of staying in touch with pressure are epidemic. Rest is something that is cast aside. The theme for today is "work hard, play hard." We don't even recognize it's a maddening world; sanity is consumed in activity.

I attended a funeral recently. In the course of the grave-side service, a plane flew over, a cell phone rang and a car alarm went off. The distractions were notable contradictions to a service honoring one who had entered his rest. Excepting the plane, the other distractions were choices.

We can choose to turn off the frenzy. Interestingly, the root word for leisure is a Latin word, *licere*, meaning "to give yourself permission." We can give ourselves permission to turn off the phone, to stop, to be quiet, and to seek God, the source of true rest. It is a difficult choice because we are addicted to frenzy. Perhaps we need a rest patch or pill—a contemporary solution to counter our addiction to frenzy, so we can rest.

Rest is important to God; he rested and commands us to as well. We are created to need sleep. Its deprivation results in irrational behavior, behavior that draws us away from His presence. God asks us to wait on Him, enabling prayer and bringing quietness to our soul. God created the day to begin with rest. We think of the day as beginning in the morning, ready to take on the world then go home and collapse. Genesis describes God's day with the words; "... and the evening and the morning were the first (second, third, etc.) day." He knew that rest comes first, even in the way He defined the day.

> Don't buy into the frenzy. Choose to practice leisure—give yourself permission to rest, God does.

16. Fear Not

And said to the mountains and rocks, Fall on us, and hide us from the face of him that sitteth on the throne, and from the wrath of the Lamb: Rev 6:16

CONTEXT

And I beheld when he had opened the sixth seal, and, lo, there was a great earthquake; and the sun became black as sackcloth of hair, and the moon became as blood; And the stars of heaven fell unto the earth, even as a fig tree casteth her untimely figs, when she is shaken of a mighty wind. And the heaven departed as a scroll when it is rolled together; and every mountain and island were moved out of their places. And the kings of the earth, and the great men, and the rich men, and the chief captains, and the mighty men, and every bondman, and every free man, hid themselves in the dens and in the rocks of the mountains; ***And said to the mountains and rocks, Fall on us, and hide us from the face of him that sitteth on the throne, and from the wrath of the Lamb:*** *For the great day of his wrath is come; and who shall be able to stand*
Rev 6:12-17

It is hard to think of our Savior as a lamb when reading the words of his great wrath. He is truly the lamb that was slain; but he is also the instrument of God's wrath. His wrath is a fearful thing; and it affects all of creation, not just mankind. Everything will be shaken. For some the shaking will be a terrible judgement. For those who are his, the judgement will be a marvelous cleansing so only the perfection of Christ's work will remain.

Over time every worldly thing is unstable. Nations and governments have come and gone, often violently. Social and economic systems sometimes change drastically. All of the things we want to trust and find our security prove unstable in the light of eternity. It is no wonder that fear is such a strong power in the world. Security flees regardless of how many locks, alarm systems and gates we erect.

God tells us not to be anxious; to cast our cares on him. Trust in the lamb of God, it is the only eternal security. Everything else fails to quench the fear that resides in our heart.

The ultimate fear is the fear of God. Regardless of how we try to temper the fear of God by defining it as awe or respect, its essence is terror, the fear of his wrath.

Who indeed shall be able to stand in the day of his wrath. There is no escape and no place to hide, except in the lamb himself. It is the lamb of God who has provided for our salvation and deliverance from his wrath.

We are still chastened, but in receiving his salvation the fear of God is revealed as the love of God. Our fear is quenched in his perfect love, and his love becomes our love for him, ourselves and our neighbor. We are safe; there is no need to hide, except in him— the rock of our salvation.

Dear Lord Jesus:

Without your salvation the fear of God comes down to wanting to be hidden from your presence. Adam hid, and those who reject you want to hide. Because of your salvation, I seek your face. I look forward to your judgement seat. I want the old stuff to be consumed in the flames of your judgement. In the meantime, I rest; but I seek your face and your work in my life. I want both your edification and your chastening. I know you love me and even hard things draw me to your provision and protection. I seek your face and you smile through the face of other believers. It is spirit seeing spirit, and I am built up.

Come, Lord Jesus

REFLECTION

One response to fear is hiding which becomes isolation. Isolation sets us up for the enemy to attack. God's plan is to fear not, rather, to be open and in unity with his body. Then there is comfort, protection and a strong defense against our enemy. Those who are not his have much to fear and there is no place to hide. Adam couldn't hide and neither can the rebellious of the world today. Every knee will bow and every tongue confess that he is Lord. Sin is horrible. It is a destructive thing which turns us from openness to the isolation of aloneness.

PRACTICE

The Westminister Catechism says the purpose of man is "to glorify God and enjoy him forever." Today it seems that doctrinal statements are tools to define a "position;" and they result in division, not unity. God has given all we need for doctrine and life in the scriptures. The precepts of man will never replace what scripture has provided, including a summary of the purpose of man having more relevance than the Catechism.

> *Let us hear the conclusion of the whole matter: Fear God, and keep his commandments: for this is the whole duty of man.*   *Eccl 12:13-14*

Unfortunately, the fear of God is badly misunderstood. It is often minimized into a sense of either respect or awe, and likened to the regard we have for highly placed or influential people. The other extreme is to turn it into some crippling terror. Neither case is true, and each greatly limits our ability to minister and be ministered to.

Francis Frangipane, pastor and author of *America at the Threshold of Destiny*, says that the reason the devil does not fear the church is that the church does not fear God. The result is ineffective ministry and even shame against the gospel of Christ.

Fear misunderstood and not applied affects our own lives as well as the Church. The enemy of our soul does not flee when resisted because we have not learned to fear God. This may not be wholly our problem. It just isn't taught; and when it is, it is watered down or used to condemn. What a shame, for this gives our enemy opportunity to counterfeit fear much like he counterfeits the other rich graces of our Lord and our God.

What makes the difference? When we choose to obey God and "fear not," God is then free to work in our lives and our circumstance. He is free to minister the grace of fearing God. The fear of God is surely a grace in much the same way that his marvelous love is a grace. Hear the words of John Newton a man who knew the *Amazing Grace* of our God.

> *Twas grace that taught my heart to fear, and grace my fears relieved.*
> *How precious did that grace appear, the hour I first believed.*

Practice learning the fear of God by choosing to "fear not." Make a list of things which you fear. This may be hard to do, because fear likes to hide. Pray, let God reveal your fear. Let him heal your fear with his love. Know that there is nothing you may have to face that he will not give sufficient grace.

17. Salvation's Voice

And cried with a loud voice, saying, Salvation to our God
which sitteth upon the throne, and unto the Lamb.

Rev 7:10

CONTEXT

*And after these things I saw four angels standing on the
four corners of the earth, holding the four winds of the
earth, that the wind should not blow on the earth, nor on
the sea, nor on any tree. And I saw another angel ascend-
ing from the east, having the seal of the living God: and he
cried with a loud voice to the four angels, to whom it was
given to hurt the earth and the sea, Saying, Hurt not the
earth, neither the sea, nor the trees, till we have sealed the
servants of our God in their foreheads. And I heard the
number of them which were sealed: and there were sealed
an hundred and forty and four thousand of all the tribes of
the children of Israel. Of the tribe of Juda were sealed
twelve thousand. Of the tribe of Reuben were sealed twelve
thousand. Of the tribe of Gad were sealed twelve thousand. Of the tribe of Aser were sealed twelve thousand. Of
the tribe of Nephthalim were sealed twelve thousand. Of
the tribe of Manasses were sealed twelve thousand. Of the
tribe of Simeon were sealed twelve thousand. Of the tribe
of Levi were sealed twelve thousand. Of the tribe of Issachar
were sealed twelve thousand. Of the tribe of Zabulon were
sealed twelve thousand. Of the tribe of Joseph were sealed
twelve thousand. Of the tribe of Benjamin were sealed
twelve thousand. After this I beheld, and, lo, a great multitude, which no man could number, of all nations, and
kindreds, and people, and tongues, stood before the throne,
and before the Lamb, clothed with white robes, and palms*

*in their hands; **And cried with a loud voice, saying, Salvation to our God which sitteth upon the throne, and unto the Lamb.*** *Rev 7:1-10*

It is a marvelous thing to consider the work of angels. Popular television programs portray them as instruments in the lives of hurting people. Gentle angels, encouraging and even conspiring to make every thing come out right within sixty minutes.

One reality of angels we would rather not face is their role as instruments of the wrath of God. Even in considering the work of wrath, we can rejoice in the peace of God, knowing he is salvation. For those who believe, the fear of God becomes the love of God as we discover we are saved from his wrath.

Another work of angels is to seal those who are identified as *the servants of our God.* A seal is a mark. It identifies both author and owner. As the body of Christ we are also sealed, but by the Holy Spirit. We were created by God and have become his property. One day some will be sealed for destruction. Praise God— his seal is greater.

> *In whom ye also trusted, after that ye heard the word of truth, the gospel of your salvation: in whom also after that ye believed, ye were sealed with that holy Spirit of promise, Which is the earnest of our inheritance until the redemption of the purchased possession, unto the praise of his glory.* *Eph 1:13-14*

Sealing is an individual process. We are not just sealed as a church; it is a personal matter and a source of joy as we realize the value of our redemption and the inheritance we have in our Lord Jesus Christ.

Sometimes I view the church as a small thing, but the redeemed are a great multitude and impossible to number. Our God is worthy of great praise, and the beneficiaries of his great salvation are a great multitude all washed by the blood of Jesus Christ and all participating in the greatness of praise. The praise is for the salvation of our God and the lamb. It will be proclaimed loudly in heaven and should be one of the loud voices of the church in the world today.

Dear Lord Jesus:

When it is all said and done, one word brings it all together—salvation. God has made it possible, and you paid the price. You, the lamb of God, died for my sins. If I have a white robe it is because of you. What a horrible price sin extracts. Hurt, pain and even *great tribulation* are all the effects of sin. You overcame the ultimate effect of sin—death. You restore us to life with robes to cover the degradation of our sin—my sin. A robe does not cover my face Lord; make it your face. Show me your glory, and let me display it in my own face.

Facing you.

REFLECTION

Salvation is worthy of being declared in a loud voice. It is a mighty picture of our God, a picture of his grace, his glory, his provision, his love, his faithfulness and other marvelous qualities. He has done the mighty work of salvation because of who he is. He made me and has redeemed me from the effects of sin. When I stand in a white robe, which is none of my doing, I will also say salvation, and do it with a loud voice. I can say salvation today, not to him, but to a world of lost individuals. To him I say "Here am I, send me." I can go in the name of Jesus, which is salvation.

PRACTICE

Are there any loud voices today? Death cries out, and we shield ourselves with hospitals and funeral homes. In doing so we lose the impact of death until we have to face it ourselves. How can we realize the horror of sin if the sting of death is removed?

Redemption cries out, but we shield ourselves by isolating "church" into religious organizations. True life is denied as we remove matters of soul and spirit from daily life. If we don't have to face death, we don't have to face redemption. The loud voice of death is quenched; and the quiet voice of redemption is unheard.

The loudest voice today seems to be a commercial, and even that loses its impact in its very prevalence. Loud voices are silenced in an ear that cannot hear, being dulled by the noise of the world. Praise to our God who speaks to us in a still small voice. It is in the stillness that we actually can hear. Somehow the deafening noise of the world only makes his still small voice unique. We have to stop to hear. It is different, it is quiet, it is truth.

Be still, and know that I am God: I will be exalted among the heathen, I will be exalted in the earth.   *Ps 46:10*

Establish a part of your daily meditation as a quiet time. Make the quiet time quiet. Usually, we pray or meditate and call it a quiet time. Remember, a quiet time is for listening or just being silent. God will be exalted loudly when we practice the praise of silence.

---

18. Salvation's Healing

For the Lamb which is in the midst of the throne shall feed them, and shall lead them unto living fountains of waters: and God shall wipe away all tears from their eyes.

Rev 7:17

CONTEXT

And all the angels stood round about the throne, and about the elders and the four beasts, and fell before the throne on their faces, and worshipped God, Saying, Amen: Blessing, and glory, and wisdom, and thanksgiving, and honour, and power, and might, be unto our God for ever and ever. Amen. And one of the elders answered, saying unto me, What are these which are arrayed in white robes? and whence came they? And I said unto him, Sir, thou knowest. And he said to me, These are they which came out of great tribulation, and have washed their robes, and made them white in the blood of the Lamb. Therefore are they before the throne of God, and serve him day and night in his temple: and he that sitteth on the throne shall dwell among them. They shall hunger no more, neither thirst any more; neither shall the sun light on them, nor any heat. **For the Lamb which is in the midst of the throne shall feed them, and shall lead them unto living fountains of waters: and God shall wipe away all tears from their eyes.**

Rev 7:11-17

We like to think of angels as exalted beings, but the truth of their character is found in humility. Humbly they serve, and humbly they worship. To worship in humility is more than just reciting the attributes of God, it is imparting them to him. The amen of the angels is to give God all blessing, glory, wisdom, thanksgiving, honor, power and might. To give these things to God means to relinquish them in their selves. Passive worship just doesn't exist in heaven and shouldn't exist on earth..

There is a multitude in heaven, clothed in white robes, who also worship and serve God in humility. Their humility is found in the washing of their robes. Clothed in filthy rags of sin we are unworthy to praise, much less to serve our holy God. It takes humility to shed our robes and leave ourselves exposed and vulnerable. It takes trust to wash our robes in his blood and see them come out spotless and white. We are not just to be given white robes, we must wash our own robes in his blood. We are not starting over in heaven. Our robes and the essence of ourselves are intact, just washed in his blood. What we are and who we are in Christ is what becomes our humility and enables us to serve.

What joy there is in this vision of heaven. There is a promise of being fed, well watered and protected. The greatest promise is—*and he that sitteth on the throne shall dwell among them.* There is no greater hope than Jesus in the midst. It is a promise that we can experience today in the body of Christ as we come together in his name. The unity and love of Christ can be seen in one another. He asks us to feed and lead one another to living waters. He asks us to wipe away the tears of others.

We rejoice and mourn as the body of Christ rejoice and mourns. It is the work of God on earth and shall become a living reality in eternity.

Dear Lord Jesus:

No more lack, no more pain, no more aloneness. Oh Lord, you are truly salvation. You not only save "from" you save "to." You lead and feed and nourish us. God wipes away the tears and former things are remembered no more. How much sin there is to forget. How much salvation there is to remember. Praise you, Lord, for a taste of that joy in this life. It is my hope of eternity. Praise to you, Lord, for showing your way and for providing the strength to walk in it.

Settled.

REFLECTION

He fed thousands on earth and will feed us all in eternity. He offered a sinner living water on earth and will leads us all to fountains of living waters. Science looks outward for signs of life, but what they look for is an environment conducive to life, one with water. No water, no life, at least not in God's image. In eternity water will be abundant and nourishing—fountains of living water. He feeds today and he leads today; it is a taste of true life—eternal life.

PRACTICE

Salvation promises healing. It is found when we let God wipe away our tears as we forgive those who hurt us. Health is found in his living water and nourishment in the Word of God; but the pathway is paved with stones of humility. There is healing, there is health in the blood of the lamb, but it is humility that brings us to the place for receiving it.

There is a lot to practicing humility and experiencing the healing of salvation. Don't be discouraged, for actually it is impossible to do. Praise to God however, he has made himself available to all who ask according to his will. The key is to recognize it cannot be done, that is the beginning of humility. The secret is to ask and receive his grace. He will give grace to praise in difficult situations, if we just ask—we know it is his will. He will be our strength and our peace if we just ask and then act as if we believe it. It is grace that heals and grace that enables humility to be expressed in this life as well as the next.

We can join the angels as they proclaim, *Blessing, and glory, and wisdom, and thanksgiving, and honour, and power, and might, be unto our God for ever and ever.* We can be the *Amen*, the living evidence of giving to God. How do we give these things to God? They seem to be his attributes, not mine. How can I give to God? I can simply become the Amen.

Blessing: speak highly of God everyday, everywhere.

Glory: let his countenance be your countenance in joy and in mourning.

Wisdom: obedience is wisdom, simply do what he asks.

Thanksgiving: count your blessings, be specific, acknowledge his grace.

Honor: give him your substance, give away something of value. Do it without recognition.

Power: speak the name of Jesus with authority but without presumption. All power is given to him.

Might: be active in ministry, lend him your strength, the might will be his.

Practice becoming an amen to the glory of God. Recognize his power in your life. There are many things reflecting his glory. The amen recognizes and gives God credit. The practice is a secret practice. Recognize the power of God, speak it only to yourself. His glory will become evident as humility does its work in your life.

19. The Gift of Prayer

And the smoke of the incense, which came with the prayers
of the saints, ascended up before God out of the angel's
hand.   Rev 8:4

CONTEXT

> *And when he had opened the seventh seal, there was si-
> lence in heaven about the space of half an hour. And I saw
> the seven angels which stood before God; and to them were
> given seven trumpets. And another angel came and stood
> at the altar, having a golden censer; and there was given
> unto him much incense, that he should offer it with the
> prayers of all saints upon the golden altar which was be-
> fore the throne. **And the smoke of the incense, which came
> with the prayers of the saints, ascended up before God
> out of the angel's hand.** And the angel took the censer,
> and filled it with fire of the altar, and cast it into the earth:
> and there were voices, and thunderings, and lightnings,
> and an earthquake.*   *Rev 8:1-5*

It seems all the revelation of God is a progressive unfolding.
The old testament focused on life, law and prophecies all pointing
to a coming king, the Lord Jesus Christ. When he came as the Son
of God it was fulfillment of God's Word and the opening of an
even greater revelation, his grace.

There was silence in heaven when Jesus fulfilled his purpose
on this earth. His death made heaven gasp; his resurrection made
heaven rejoice. The mighty works of God should also leave us
speechless and filled with awe. Seeing his love expressed should
cause us to bow down in worship and praise.

Seven angels in the first section of Revelation were sent to
address seven churches—churches with a calling to proclaim God's

grace. Now the trumpets of the angels are to proclaim his judgement. But even the proclamation and implementation of judgement is centered around his love and the prayers of those who have chosen to receive his love, the saints of God.

What a privilege we have in prayer. Like singing it may be a unique gift to mankind, one which differentiates us from the rest of creation. Singing and praise enable us to honor God; prayer enables us to enter into a personal relationship with him. Without communication between parties there is no living vibrant relationship. Prayer is the gift God has given so we may know him. The love of God is amazing, but the experience of it on a personal level is astounding. Prayer enables communication and the substance of the relationship is the love of God.

The reality of prayer also becomes evident because it is answered. The prayer of the saints results in judgement; the vengeance of God on behalf of his saints. We often don't connect an answer to prayer with the original prayer, but he is faithful to answer, nonetheless.

Dear Lord Jesus:

Pray, pray, pray, it is like incense before God. Just consider how many have been praying for so long, Lord. The amount of prayer that has been prayed "in your name" is not small. Oh Lord Jesus, thank you for the gift of prayer. Thank you that it will be an offering before our God in eternity. Thank you, Lord, for the Holy Spirit who helps me to pray prayers that are filled with life and truth. Thank you, Lord, for the privilege to pray in your name.

In your name.

REFLECTION

Praise enlarges the habitation of God; and prayer makes it beautiful. He is the Lord and is destined to be honored by his creation. Creation praises and people pray; all give glory to God. Praise and prayer are not natural to my fallen self—I choose to praise, I choose to pray. In my self, none of it makes any sense. In my spirit, it not only makes sense, it is life. The privilege of prayer is special. Creation praises and angels praise; but we can praise and pray. It is a way to touch God, even from our fallen place.

PRACTICE

Singing and prayer seem to be gifts unique to us humans. Like most qualities they are passive until applied or even misapplied. The psalmist calls the prayer of the wicked, sin (Psalm 109:7). The world can turn song into sadness and prayer into ridicule. Most religions exercise spiritual disciplines; they fast, meditate and even say prayers. Often the prayer of the religious appears to be answered by finding inner peace or rest. There is one prayer of the wicked that is not sin, in fact, it may be the most powerful prayer on earth. It is the prayer of salvation. When an unbeliever prays to the living God and receives the salvation offered in his only Son, Jesus Christ, the whole of heaven rejoices.

After having received the grace of his wonderful salvation, prayer should become a way of life. The Scripture asks us to pray without ceasing (1 Thess 5:17). Prayer is the power that makes the love of God bilateral. He commands us to love him and prayer is a verbal expression of that love. He asks us, like he did of Peter, *do you love me?* Can I be silent? No, I must respond in prayer and a lifestyle that makes his love a reality.

Like most spiritual disciplines, prayer is not natural. The world, the flesh and the devil all conspire to destroy my prayer life and to hinder the prayers of the saints. It takes time to develop a habit, especially one which will be resisted in the spirit as well as the flesh.

Effective prayer life also involves defensive work because prayer is not natural. Take note of what hinders or keeps you from prayer. Little distractions can do great damage; but when they are exposed their power to disrupt our prayers is lost. Don't allow the enemy of your soul to distract you from the most powerful element of your life—an open relationship with father God. It is his pleasure as well as ours, as it was in the beginning, in the garden.

> To practice a life of prayer, become conscious of praying. Notice how often you pray. Keep track of prayer times. I like to write prayers to Jesus; it seems to formalize the process. Set times to pray, then spontaneous prayer will become more natural. Make it a routine to pray every morning and every evening. Read the prayers of David in the Psalms. Read them to God, he loves his word and so will we as they becomes our prayer.

20. Facing Uncertainty

And the seven angels which had the seven trumpets prepared themselves to sound.   Rev 8:6

CONTEXT

And the seven angels which had the seven trumpets pre-
pared themselves to sound. The first angel sounded, and
there followed hail and fire mingled with blood, and they
were cast upon the earth: and the third part of trees was
burnt up, and all green grass was burnt up. And the sec-
ond angel sounded, and as it were a great mountain burn-
ing with fire was cast into the sea: and the third part of the
sea became blood; And the third part of the creatures which
were in the sea, and had life, died; and the third part of the
ships were destroyed. And the third angel sounded, and
there fell a great star from heaven, burning as it were a
lamp, and it fell upon the third part of the rivers, and upon
the fountains of waters; And the name of the star is called
Wormwood: and the third part of the waters became worm-
wood; and many men died of the waters, because they were
made bitter. And the fourth angel sounded, and the third
part of the sun was smitten, and the third part of the moon,
and the third part of the stars; so as the third part of them
was darkened, and the day shone not for a third part of it,
and the night likewise. And I beheld, and heard an angel
flying through the midst of heaven, saying with a loud voice,
Woe, woe, woe, to the inhabiters of the earth by reason of
the other voices of the trumpet of the three angels, which
are yet to sound!   *Rev 8:6-13*

Angels may not sing the song of the redeemed but they sure
play a mean trumpet. Unfortunately, these are trumpets of judgement. The terrible fruit of refusing the grace of salvation.

Fortunately, there will also be a trumpet announcing resurrection.

*In a moment, in the twinkling of an eye, at the last trump:
for the trumpet shall sound, and the dead shall be raised
incorruptible, and we shall be changed.*   *1 Cor 15:52*

There is much uncertainty in the world but two things are certain: sin shall be judged and there is a resurrection. Even in the midst of horrible woe there is hope. God has a plan of redeeming love and in it even judgment mysteriously becomes a reflection of his faithfulness and a source of hope for those who enter into his grace.

The impact of these trumpets is judgement touching our world. Even today, the horror of sin's judgment is apparent. The natural world groans with environmental stress. Storms rage on the seas and pollution poisons the waters of the land. Even the sun and moon are obscured in clouds of smoke. These, however, are not judgment, just the natural consequence of sin and of a world cursed in the garden as a result of man's disobedience.

We live in a marvelously created world which is able to absorb and heal itself of the abuse of irresponsible dominion—sin. The result is woe today and a dreadful anticipation of the future. Even those with patently optimistic outlooks know that sin shall be judged. The anticipation is woe, woe, woe; but hope is in God's salvation—Jesus Christ.

Dear Lord Jesus:

Sin exists and shall be judged. You have redeemed me and made me yours. You lift me up and make me your own. You take on yourself the judgement of sin, which is death. Yet, I must die also. There is a sense in this life where I must die to my sinful self in order to live in your life. There will come a time when I will face death in the flesh. It will be hard, it will be experiencing death, but it will only be a passage to the life you have given me. I

94

love this life and the life you have given me in it. I shall love the next even more.

Loved, loving.

REFLECTION

John saw seven angels with seven trumpets, preparing to sound. I wonder how he felt. Today there are many proclaiming imminent doom and impending judgement—but life goes on. What John saw was reality and he told it like he saw it. I wonder what the doom-saying prophets of today see, or imagine, or wish. Is it fear or arrogance? It is no doubt that the time of God's judgement will come. It is necessary or his time of full restoration cannot come. We have a shadow of judgement and of restoration today, but the eternal plan will unfold in God's own time.

PRACTICE

Two of the snares of life are, to be bound by a regretful past, or to be anxious about the future. Even if we can avoid the snares and live the life God has given for today, we are often discontent. It seems that in every phase of life we are looking for the next step. As a child in school I always looked forward to the next grade. Nothing was ever finished. Completing elementary school was really just the beginning of middle school. Things will be better when I learn to drive, graduate from high school, start college, begin a career, family, buy a home, or pay it off.

The list seems endless and filled with uncertainty that is really a reflection of discontent. The Bible instructs us to be content and in so doing there is great gain (1 Tim 6:6-8). Both anxiety over the future and placing all my hope in the future will rob me of today. One thing I fear is coming to the end of life saying, "where did all the time go." I would rather look back and say, I have run a good race.

We often quote the end of Hebrews 13:5; in fact, *I will never leave thee, nor forsake thee* was my anchor during a dark period of my life. The essence of the verse, however, may be in it's opening phrases.

> *Let your conversation be without covetousness; and be content with such things as ye have: for he hath said, I will never leave thee, nor forsake thee.*　　　　*Heb 13:5*

Contentment comes in the firm knowledge that Jesus will never leave nor forsake us. I can acquire contentment by continuously focusing on his commitment to be with me in good and bad times. Past regrets are erased in his loving forgiveness; and future anxiety is quenched in the assurance of his loving presence and care.

To practice contentment remember the past, hope in the future, but live in today. Take time today to appreciate this day, even if it is a small thing like a sunset or a meal with a friend. Remember, abundant life is for today.

---

21. Enduring Difficulty

One woe is past; and, behold, there come two woes more
hereafter.   Rev 9:12

CONTEXT:

*And the fifth angel sounded, and I saw a star fall from
heaven unto the earth: and to him was given the key of the
bottomless pit. And he opened the bottomless pit; and there
arose a smoke out of the pit, as the smoke of a great furnace; and the sun and the air were darkened by reason of
the smoke of the pit. And there came out of the smoke
locusts upon the earth: and unto them was given power, as
the scorpions of the earth have power. And it was commanded them that they should not hurt the grass of the
earth, neither any green thing, neither any tree; but only
those men which have not the seal of God in their foreheads. And to them it was given that they should not kill
them, but that they should be tormented five months: and
their torment was as the torment of a scorpion, when he
striketh a man. And in those days shall men seek death,
and shall not find it; and shall desire to die, and death
shall flee from them. And the shapes of the locusts were
like unto horses prepared unto battle; and on their heads
were as it were crowns like gold, and their faces were as
the faces of men. And they had hair as the hair of women,
and their teeth were as the teeth of lions. And they had
breastplates, as it were breastplates of iron; and the sound
of their wings was as the sound of chariots of many horses
running to battle. And they had tails like unto scorpions,
and there were stings in their tails: and their power was to
hurt men five months. And they had a king over them,
which is the angel of the bottomless pit, whose name in the
Hebrew tongue is Abaddon, but in the Greek tongue hath*

his name Apollyon. **One woe is past; and, behold, there come two woes more hereafter** *Rev 9:1-12*

If I were not a Christian it would be hard to read these passages, except that it might cause me to believe unto salvation. The only consolation of woes is that they are under the control of God. No angel of hell, nor any demon has any authority except through God. I can rest in his love and even find his faithfulness in the assurance that evil—sin—will be horribly judged.

There is chastening for those who are sealed to God, but no torment nor destructive judgment. I can bring destruction into my own life through poor or sinful choices, but the God who loves me has a mysterious way of turning even that to my good.

> *For our light affliction, which is but for a moment, worketh for us a far more exceeding and eternal weight of glory;*
> *2 Cor 4:17*

For those who reject the grace of God the blessing of hope vanishes; only a certain fearful looking for of judgment and fiery indignation remains (Heb 10:27).

Perhaps the hardest part of woes for a believer is the sadness it brings, knowing that those who suffer the woes of judgment could have escaped if only they had accepted the love of God in Christ. For me, difficulty can be endured with patience; but my heart is broken for those without hope.

Dear Lord Jesus:

Life in the flesh is one woe after another. It is hard to live life in rebellion to God. Praise to you Lord, for giving strength to overcome and blessing to see beyond woes. You are the Lord and even woes are designed for my good. They are designed to turn me to repentance and teach me the fear of God. Thank you, Lord, for saving me from the effect of these woes, but loving me enough to let me experience the horror of my own sin. It taught me to hate sin and its effect. You are the Lord; you are my Lord. Nothing happens except you allow it and turn it for my good.

Very loved.

REFLECTION

Woes come, some I bring on myself, some just come. I have plenty to pray about when I focus on circumstances. Deliver me, help me to walk through hard times—these are perpetual prayer requests. One need passes only to be replaced by another. Instead of focusing on needs, events or circumstances, I can concentrate on my Lord, Jesus Christ. Then circumstances will be just part of life. Life has been called a journey, and it is. All of it is to be experienced, even woes. If they are experienced in Christ, they are not points of despair, but points of overcoming.

PRACTICE

A delightful meditative book entitled *Benedict's Way*, speaks of perseverance. The book quotes an inscription found on a cellar wall in Cologne, Germany, where Jews hid from the Nazis.

I believe in the sun even when it is not shining.
I believe in love even when feeling it not.
I believe in God even when he is silent.

Like love, enduring difficulty is a decision—a choice. It is not based on feelings although they may be a source of the strength to decide to endure. Having made a decision to endure, it may seem to be impossible to perform. One of the destructive qualities of pain and suffering is discouragement. Some woes make it seem like death is the only resolution. That is why we must practice to endure difficulty.

Waiting until difficulty intrudes into life may be too late, the pressure may be overwhelming. Difficulty will always intrude; it is not a gentleman, it does not wait for a convenient time.

A marathoner trains to endure the pain of running while tired. Marines train to endure the intensity of combat. The question is, how do you train do endure difficulty? Surely it is not to purposely walk into difficult situations. No, the way to train to endure is to train to trust the God who allows difficulty.

> The journal of his faithfulness is the training manual for this exercise. Remember his faithfulness during a particularly difficult time in the past. Be specific about how you felt and the choices you made which enabled endurance. Pray, ask God what he is building in your life through what he has allowed in your life. You are his—trust him!

22. Blessed Repentance

And the rest of the men which were not killed by these
plagues yet repented not of the works of their hands, ...

Rev 9:20a

CONTEXT

*And the sixth angel sounded, and I heard a voice from the
four horns of the golden altar which is before God, Saying
to the sixth angel which had the trumpet, Loose the four
angels which are bound in the great river Euphrates. And
the four angels were loosed, which were prepared for an
hour, and a day, and a month, and a year, for to slay the
third part of men. And the number of the army of the horse-
men were two hundred thousand thousand: and I heard
the number of them. And thus I saw the horses in the vision, and them that sat on them, having breastplates of
fire, and of jacinth, and brimstone: and the heads of the
horses were as the heads of lions; and out of their mouths
issued fire and smoke and brimstone. By these three was
the third part of men killed, by the fire, and by the smoke,
and by the brimstone, which issued out of their mouths.
For their power is in their mouth, and in their tails: for
their tails were like unto serpents, and had heads, and with
them they do hurt.* **And the rest of the men which were
not killed by these plagues yet repented not of the works
of their hands,** *that they should not worship devils, and
idols of gold, and silver, and brass, and stone, and of wood:
which neither can see, nor hear, nor walk: Neither repented
they of their murders, nor of their sorceries, nor of their
fornication, nor of their thefts.*   *Rev 9:13-21*

One of the dangers of Christian living is to take the works of our enemy casually. Satan hates me and wants to destroy my witness and my life. He has authority on the earth, although it is constrained by God. Nevertheless, our enemy is like a roaring loin, seeking whom he may devour. Death and destruction are his calling cards; and his ruthlessness is toward all of mankind, not just believers.

Those who are released to implement the judgment of God are numerous, zealous and well-equipped. Our strength is in God and we can be equally numerous and unified in his Holy Spirit. We can be equally zealous in purpose and conviction. We can be equally equipped in the knowledge of the truth by God's Holy Word. Our strength is magnified in the Lord because he is greater than any created power in the earth. We may be little, but we are of God.

Ye are of God, little children, and have overcome them: because greater is he that is in you, than he that is in the world.   *I Jn 4:4*

The ruthlessness of sin is not restrained on those who are not of God. Those who have chosen to reject his grace place themselves in the path of his judgement. Shadows of these judgments exist today. Large scale death is not new to the world. War, famine, plague and natural disasters are part of our ancient and recent history.

It seems that all of mankind would run to God for his salvation, but even with terrible judgment, natural man rejects God. Impenitency is likely to be the most horrible consequence of sin because it fulfills the end of sin—death.

Dear Lord Jesus:

Woes and horrible circumstances, just don't bring repentance. What does? Could it be love? Could it be that knowing you love me draws me to repentance? Without love, woeful circumstances may only brings bitterness. Thank you, Lord, that you have always loved me, even in my points of rebellion; even in my lowest moments. How great is your love for me, Lord. Thank you for drawing me to repentance. Thank you for teaching me the fear of God so that I will choose to stay in the richness of your love. Praise to you, Lord; you are indeed love.

Loved at all times.

REFLECTION

In the history of Israel, woes and terrible circumstances often brought repentance. The reason may be because they knew they were God's people and had experienced his mighty acts. They could connect their circumstance to their relationship with God. Unfortunately, blessing often brought backsliding and another cycle of woes. If repentance does not come from woes it must be because people don't, or won't, see the connection. If God is irrelevant in life then his hand will be unseen in circumstances. God haters or God ignorers will not find the joy of repentance. Praise to my God for teaching me his love—for loving me in both hard and easy times. I want circumstances to be irrelevant, not God. I want to be sensitive to his ways, not his works.

PRACTICE

Repentance is a joyful process, a gift from God to enable our return to an awareness of his blessing. He is always a blessing to those who are his, but the darkness of our impenitence clouds his love and care. Repentance turns us to the light. When we are turned from his light, we are in the darkness of our own shadow.

I can not understand why we choose the darkness, yet I do it so often. The light is so refreshing, so enlightening, so comforting. Why would anyone choose to stay in the dark? Still the power of darkness resides in our flesh. It takes time for repentance to become a natural part of life. We can pray with the psalmist: *Search me, O God, and know my heart: try me, and know my thoughts: And see if there be any wicked way in me, and lead me in the way everlasting* (Ps 139:23-24).

The issue is what will we do when the wicked ways are revealed. The only reasonable response is repentance. Confessing may be agreeing with God what he reveals is true, but repentance is obedience to God. It will allow salvation to do its perfect work in life.

> *Wherefore, my beloved, as ye have always obeyed, not as in my presence only, but now much more in my absence, work out your own salvation with fear and trembling. For it is God which worketh in you both to will and to do of his good pleasure.* Phil 2:12-13

Practice repentance, pray with God to reveal the darkness in you. His light reveals but it is our responsibility to respond. There is, and always will be, plenty to repent of. The blessing of repentance will be a daily blessing, if it is allowed to become a habit.

23. Mystery Revealed

But in the days of the voice of the seventh angel, when he shall begin to sound, the mystery of God should be finished, as he hath declared to his servants the prophets.

Rev 10:7

CONTEXT

And I saw another mighty angel come down from heaven, clothed with a cloud: and a rainbow was upon his head, and his face was as it were the sun, and his feet as pillars of fire: And he had in his hand a little book open: and he set his right foot upon the sea, and his left foot on the earth, And cried with a loud voice, as when a lion roareth: and when he had cried, seven thunders uttered their voices. And when the seven thunders had uttered their voices, I was about to write: and I heard a voice from heaven saying unto me, Seal up those things which the seven thunders uttered, and write them not. And the angel which I saw stand upon the sea and upon the earth lifted up his hand to heaven, And sware by him that liveth for ever and ever, who created heaven, and the things that therein are, and the earth, and the things that therein are, and the sea, and the things which are therein, that there should be time no longer: **But in the days of the voice of the seventh angel, when he shall begin to sound, the mystery of God should be finished, as he hath declared to his servants the prophets.** *And the voice which I heard from heaven spake unto me again, and said, Go and take the little book which is open in the hand of the angel which standeth upon the sea and upon the earth. And I went unto the angel, and said unto him, Give me the little book. And he said unto me, Take it, and eat it up; and it shall make thy belly bitter, but it shall be in thy mouth sweet as honey. And I took the* *little book out of the angel's hand, and ate it up; and it was in my mouth sweet as honey: and as soon as I had eaten it, my belly was bitter. And he said unto me, Thou must prophesy again before many peoples, and nations, and tongues, and kings.*   *Rev 10:1-11*

Sometimes the Word of God, Scripture, is overwhelming in its description of the things of God. Like John's description of the mighty angel, it is glorious, powerful and beautiful. It is just a little book, but it roars with truth. How else would God describe the horrors of sin except through stories of those with its affliction? How else would God reveal the mysteries of the kingdom of heaven but with stories which our limited minds can understand and relate to? Yet, even within the great revelation of Scripture, there is mystery. There is mystery because it is not God's time for the fullness of revelation. There is mystery because his essence is beyond our finite comprehension.

The mystery of God's plan of redemption became clear when he chose to become a man in Christ Jesus. The mystery of his restoration will also have a time where we shall hear, "it is finished," and everything will then become reality. Even the timelessness of eternity will be understood and enjoyed.

In the meantime, we can consume the little book of both bitter and sweet truth. We can learn to recognize the bitterness of sin and praise him for the sweetness of redemption. Then it will become our own bittersweet testimony to proclaim.

Dear Lord Jesus:

You seem to be a mystery, Lord, but you are a revelation. You are the mystery of God and also his revelation. You show in your life and death the great mystery of how much God loves the world and more specifically, how he loves me. Thank you, Lord, for opening the words spoken in mystery by the prophets. Thank you, Lord, for letting me see through a glass darkly. Thank you for the hope of seeing clearly in that day. There seems to be a great mystery, but in reality, it is just my blindness.

Seeing your openness.

REFLECTION

My Lord said "It is finished," and the mystery of God's plan for redemption was completed. The mystery of his restoration continues as the Holy Spirit does his work of convicting and conforming. Praise to my God who has always loved me and who is restoring me in, and to, that love. Many things are finished; and his love continues to work in completing even more. One day it will all come together, but for now it is still a mystery. There is much that we will not know until the day of Jesus Christ, but what he has revealed we can know. He has revealed himself.

PRACTICE

Scripture is not a mystery. In it God has revealed himself to the fullest extent we can understand. Through the telescope of Scripture we find the glorious nature of God in all his splendor. Through the microscope of Scripture we find our own broken selves. Through the open words of Scripture we find the plan of salvation and the invitation to consume the words.

God's Word is life and must be consumed to become our life. How can I speak of the love of God except that I first experience it? How can I speak of the fear of God except that I have come to tremble before it? The testimony of Scripture is passive until it is consumed. Then it becomes life.

Let the word of Christ dwell in you richly in all wisdom; teaching and admonishing one another in psalms and hymns and spiritual songs, singing with grace in your hearts to the Lord.   Col 3:16

The word of God is meant to dwell in people who make up the body of Christ. It is meant to give us life and to compel us to express that life to one another and to the world. The world has no problem discounting Scripture when it is just a book. When it has become life, it must be either resisted or ignored. Both responses exist today. Christians are resisted and killed for their faith. In our culture the other response prevails, Christians are ignored as irrelevant. The book, the Bible, continues to be a best seller, but its living words often stay on the shelf.

Practice the revelation of God's greatest mystery to the world—his salvation. If you have never done it write out your testimony. Even if you never share it, let it become life. The plan of salvation may be ignored, but a transformed life will have to be resisted or believed.

24. Measuring Up

And there was given me a reed like unto a rod: and the angel stood, saying, Rise, and measure the temple of God, and the altar, and them that worship therein.   Rev 11:1

CONTEXT

And there was given me a reed like unto a rod: and the angel stood, saying, Rise, and measure the temple of God, and the altar, and them that worship therein. But the court which is without the temple leave out, and measure it not; for it is given unto the Gentiles: and the holy city shall they tread under foot forty and two months. And I will give power unto my two witnesses, and they shall prophesy a thousand two hundred and threescore days, clothed in sackcloth. These are the two olive trees, and the two candlesticks standing before the God of the earth. And if any man will hurt them, fire proceedeth out of their mouth, and devoureth their enemies: and if any man will hurt them, he must in this manner be killed. These have power to shut heaven, that it rain not in the days of their prophecy: and have power over waters to turn them to blood, and to smite the earth with all plagues, as often as they will. And when they shall have finished their testimony, the beast that ascendeth out of the bottomless pit shall make war against them, and shall overcome them, and kill them. And their dead bodies shall lie in the street of the great city, which spiritually is called Sodom and Egypt, where also our Lord was crucified. And they of the people and kindreds and tongues and nations shall see their dead bodies three days and an half, and shall not suffer their dead bodies to be put in graves. And they that dwell upon the earth shall rejoice over them, and make merry, and shall send gifts one to another; because these two prophets tormented them

*that dwelt on the earth. And after three days and an half
the Spirit of life from God entered into them, and they stood
upon their feet; and great fear fell upon them which saw
them. And they heard a great voice from heaven saying
unto them, Come up hither. And they ascended up to heaven
in a cloud; and their enemies beheld them. And the same
hour was there a great earthquake, and the tenth part of
the city fell, and in the earthquake were slain of men seven
thousand: and the remnant were affrighted, and gave glory
to the God of heaven.* *Rev 11:1-13*

Why should we try to measure spiritual things? What measurements are appropriate? Left to us, we will count attendance or giving; but God has a measure for us. His rod measures our compassion, care and love. Spiritual measurement has a purpose beyond just knowing where we stand. We are measured for preservation from the world, for restoration from our fallen place, for trials and testimony, and frequently for reformation from doctrinal and practice error.

We are called to measure the church, test our worship and examine the body of Christ. We are not called to measure the world, it is beyond spiritual measurement. We are inadequate to judge the body of Christ; how can we expect to apply spiritual measures to those who are not spiritual?

We cannot measure results. If we knew the blessings that come from expressing his love, we would surely become arrogant. A shoe clerk shared his faith with a customer, the customer shared his testimony and after several more cycles a man name Billy Graham gave his life to the Lord. The shoe clerk never knew his testimony would result in salvation for millions.

It doesn't take many witnesses to change the world. Only two are required. Jesus said, *in the mouth of two or three witnesses every word may be established* (Matt 18:16). Like voting, every witness counts; and we cannot relinquish our responsibility to others. It is amazing what the effect of one testimony can be in the hands of our living God.

Dear Lord Jesus:

How do we measure the church, Lord? You are the Lord of the church; you are the one who gives life to the church and it becomes your body. John was told to measure the temple, the altar and the people. I see your body as people, Lord. I see the church as a structure, a realm of authority. The world looks at the church and often sees lack, hurt, division and are turned from the things of God. People's lives changed by God become the true testimony of your life. Help me to use a proper measure, Lord.

Accountable

REFLECTION

My body is a temple to the Lord, and my heart is its altar. How do they measure up? Is my health okay? Do I practice good eating habits and find both exercise and rest? I can measure physical attributes, but how about the altar—it is more deceptive? What I worship is even trickier to discern? I pray for God to search me, try me, and see if there be any wicked way in me. This searching has been difficult because it often reveals the depth of my sin. He has restored me and even allowed me to share his love again. Yet the darkness remains; but now it is bound in his fear. I can live daily in his love and fear, and it is not a contradiction.

PRACTICE

How many hours do I pray? How do I tithe? How many of the sick did I visit? These and many others are all things that can be measured, but are they measures of the spirit?

> *He hath shewed thee, O man, what is good; and what doth the LORD require of thee, but to do justly, and to love mercy, and to walk humbly with thy God?*   *Micah 6:8*

How on earth do we measure these things? On earth we don't, they are spiritual. We cannot be trusted to measure them, it will become legalism. The other extreme is to proclaim spiritual matters as unmeasurable. This can result in carelessness and even apathy about the things of God.

We are called to love, to minister, to care and there should be ways to tell if we are being successful so we will hear, *Well done, thou good and faithful servant, ... enter thou into the joy of thy lord* (Matt 25:21).

Practice measuring up by relaxing in the spirit and asking God to measure your heart. Measure what you can manage. Purposely choose godly thoughts—*whatsoever things are true, whatsoever things are honest, whatsoever things are just, whatsoever things are pure, whatsoever things are lovely, whatsoever things are of good report; if there be any virtue, and if there be any praise, think on these things* (Phil 4:8).

---

25. A Heavenly Reward

... and that thou shouldest give reward unto thy servants the prophets, and to the saints, and them that fear thy name, small and great; ...   Rev 11:18p

CONTEXT

*The second woe is past; and, behold, the third woe cometh quickly. And the seventh angel sounded; and there were great voices in heaven, saying, The kingdoms of this world are become the kingdoms of our Lord, and of his Christ; and he shall reign for ever and ever. And the four and twenty elders, which sat before God on their seats, fell upon their faces, and worshipped God, Saying, We give thee thanks, O Lord God Almighty, which art, and wast, and art to come; because thou hast taken to thee thy great power, and hast reigned. And the nations were angry, and thy wrath is come, and the time of the dead, that they should be judged, **and that thou shouldest give reward unto thy servants the prophets, and to the saints, and them that fear thy name, small and great;** and shouldest destroy them which destroy the earth. And the temple of God was opened in heaven, and there was seen in his temple the ark of his testament: and there were lightnings, and voices, and thunderings, and an earthquake, and great hail.*
Rev 11:14-19

The good news of the gospel was to announce the kingdom of heaven was at hand. Kingdom living was near and available to those who would enter into the promise of his grace. The reality of kingdom living is a cause for worship. It is an appropriate response to recognizing the eternity of Christ's kingdom in eternity past, present and future.

Even the judgment of Christ is a time of rejoicing. We can rejoice in his faithfulness to his word. He is faithful to destroy sin and to reward those who fear his name. The fear of God is a glorious thing. It draws us to his love and turns us from the snares of sin in this life. God spoke to Abram proclaiming himself to be his great reward (Gen 15:1). The psalmist calls the Word of God a source of great reward, if it is kept (Psalm 19:8-11). Jesus called enduring patience a source of great heavenly reward and something to rejoice over in this life (Matt 5:11-12). The presence of God in Christ is the greatest reward we can have in this life, the next, and forever.

In heaven the temple of God is open; and the temple of our lives should be open today. We can pray—*Thy kingdom come. Thy will be done in earth, as it is in heaven* (Matt 6:10). The reality of this prayer could be in reflecting his love and care in this life.

Dear Lord Jesus:

There is only one reward; it is you, Lord. Praise you for overcoming and for taking your place in the body of those who love you. Thank you, Lord, that you reward the small and the great. Count me among those who fear your name, Lord. Great things do not appear to be my calling, but I know that you have used me. Thank you, Lord, for finding me, for waiting through my rebellion and for teaching me to be in the fear of your name. It is love Lord, and that is a reward in itself.

Small among the great.

REFLECTION

The verse speaks of reward as if it is solitary, but it is richly manifold. The reward is Christ, but it shows in the Scripture, in life, in Spirit, in the body of Christ and in relationships. Ultimately it will all be completed and fulfilled in Christ. It is in the love of God and in the fear of God. It is in his glory and in his wrath. Everything God does is good, because he is good. I do not deserve any reward, except that he has allowed me to enter in, to be a part of the heavenly reward. He has given me salvation and is giving me life in his Spirit. It is more that a reward, it is love.

PRACTICE

The beatitudes tell us that there is blessing in spiritual poverty, mourning, meekness, seeking of righteousness, mercy, purity of heart, peacemaking, and both physical and emotional persecution in the name of Jesus (Matt 5:3-11). The world says this is foolishness and our fleshly nature agrees with the world. It is this very contradiction with worldly wisdom which embraces the heavenly blessing. Living the contradiction enables God's blessing to be experienced even in this life.

In a very real way we choose both blessing and cursing. Our attitudes and choices all have consequences of both temporal and eternal value. Moses said that it was ail before us, and he admonished us to *choose life.*

> *I call heaven and earth to record this day against you, that I have set before you life and death, blessing and cursing: therefore choose life, that both thou and thy seed may live: That thou mayest love the LORD thy God, and that thou mayest obey his voice, and that thou mayest cleave unto him: for he is thy life, and the length of thy days: ...*
> *Deut 30:19-20*

Does this mean we should seek to be poor or continually mourn or debase ourselves? No, the heavenly blessing is in choosing life and in recognizing that God is the source of life. We can seek righteousness, practice mercy, make peace and pray for those who hurt us. Those are choices that let God's glory show in our countenance. Recognizing our spiritual poverty should only cause us to seek the Lord and his presence.

I am amazed at modern advertising which projects the good life, especially in style and fashion. I notice none of the models smile. The acceptable countenance of the world seems to be a smirk, frown or a seductive look. One time while jogging in a busy city I decided to smile and speak a greeting to everyone I saw. The reactions varied from fear to surprise. A few even responded with blessing. Regardless of the response, I was blessed with heavenly reward.

We can begin to practice the heavenly reward on earth by our countenance. A smile may be the way others can see that there is something of heaven in us. We are, after all the body of Christ on earth. The kingdom of heaven is at hand and we are its handiwork—let it show.

26. The Pain of Life

> And she being with child cried, travailing in birth, and
> pained to be delivered.   Rev 12:2

CONTEXT

> *And there appeared a great wonder in heaven; a woman*
> *clothed with the sun, and the moon under her feet, and*
> *upon her head a crown of twelve stars:* ***And she being***
> ***with child cried, travailing in birth, and pained to be de-***
> ***livered.*** *And there appeared another wonder in heaven;*
> *and behold a great red dragon, having seven heads and*
> *ten horns, and seven crowns upon his heads. And his tail*
> *drew the third part of the stars of heaven, and did cast*
> *them to the earth: and the dragon stood before the woman*
> *which was ready to be delivered, for to devour her child as*
> *soon as it was born. And she brought forth a man child,*
> *who was to rule all nations with a rod of iron: and her*
> *child was caught up unto God, and to his throne. And the*
> *woman fled into the wilderness, where she hath a place*
> *prepared of God, that they should feed her there a thou-*
> *sand two hundred and threescore days.*   Rev 12:1-6

The wonders of heaven appear mysterious and grand, but they
are afflicted with problems which often seem commonplace in the
earth. The pain of childbirth has been a part of life since God
judged the woman as a result of the fall.

> *To the woman he said, "I will greatly increase your pains*
> *in childbearing; with pain you will give birth to children.*
> *Your desire will be for your husband, and he will rule over*
> *you."*   Gen 3:16

This was a judgement, not a curse, and even the judgement may not be considered a punishment, if viewed from an eternal perspective. While pronouncing judgement, God is imparting himself to those whom he loves. It is God's Son who will feel the pain of human birth so that he can be like us—tempted in every way, yet without sin. It is he who will submit to his Father's will and therefore to worldly authority, even unto death—for our salvation.

The conflict between woman and the serpent were also part of this original garden judgement, setting up the strife which we all experience in the wilderness of life.

> *And I will put enmity between thee and the woman, and*
> *between thy seed and her seed; it shall bruise thy head,*
> *and thou shalt bruise his heel.*   *Gen 3:15*

God's judgement is a place where we learn of our desperate need for his salvation, protected from eternal destruction and kept for the glory of God.

Dear Lord Jesus:

You were born to pain and travail. The world is still in pain and travail, and the enemy of God wanted to destroy you and harm us. You have overcome and God will prevail. I am a part of that remnant which is in your overcoming. Praise you, Lord, for what has been; it is the basis for my faith. Praise you, Lord, for what will be; it is where I find hope. Thank you, Lord, for what is, for that is where I find love. You are the Lord of glory and somehow you love enough to show me your glory—it is your love in those who love you.

                                        Pained in life.

REFLECTION

Life is filled with pain and my Lord still chose life. He faced and overcame temptation, so that I might find salvation. Most of my pain I bring on myself, although there is plenty of unsolicited pain to go around. Happiness may be quenched in the pain of life, but joy is something I can enter. Jesus says, enter into my joy. I don't even know how to do this. I pray the Lord will show me his joy, joy that is independent of circumstance. I think I know peace in circumstance but perhaps it is just apathy. I believe I know love and have experienced its unconditional nature. All of these, love, joy and peace are bounties of the Holy Spirit.

PRACTICE

In the mid 70's Francis A. Schaeffer, a noted evangelical thinker, published a book entitled *How Should We Then Live?* The title reflects our own challenge to be free from the condemnation of a curse and free to live in the love of God even in the wilderness.

In the garden, a choice was necessary; and it is no different today. That choice is to believe the truth—to enter into the grace of his salvation and to be born of the spirit. Then the love of God can do its work of redemption and restoration. Having entered in, then the process of allowing God to work begins.

Knowing the truth of not being cursed can release us from spiritual, emotional and even physical problems. We can choose to walk each day in the light as he is in the light (I John 1:7). Then we experience the power to break the bondage of sin that he has canceled by his own blood.

Being free from bondage and experiencing the healing it brings is only part of the great provision he has made for us. We also have the power to live in his love (Ephesians 3:14-19). Then our healing becomes ministry so that others can enter into his redemption and restoration. The great commandment becomes the great commission. When the lawyer discerned who his neighbor was, after hearing the good Samaritan story (Luke 10:37), Jesus told him "Go and do likewise." Our charge and our blessing is nothing less.

Practice living freely in the wilderness, not bound to sin but free to love God, yourself and your neighbor. Wilderness can result in despair at the pain of life; but realizing it is God's protection allows us the freedom to minister his love even in painful times. Joyce Landorf, a noted bible teacher and author, tells of her mother's words as she was approaching the end of her journey. She said, "I have taught you to live as a Christian, Now I will teach you how to die as one." These are powerful words to us who struggle, who hurt and who suffer.

We need to practice letting our pain be a testimony of enduring love. There are many who are suffering today. Scripture says to weep with those who weep (Rom 12:15). Spend some time with the sick or infirmed. Visit a nursing home or hospital. Just listen and comfort. Don't preach or try to heal, just mourn with them.

---

27. Facing the Accuser

And I heard a loud voice saying in heaven, Now is come salvation, and strength, and the kingdom of our God, and the power of his Christ: for the accuser of our brethren is cast down, which accused them before our God day and night.   Rev 12:10

CONTEXT

And there was war in heaven: Michael and his angels fought against the dragon; and the dragon fought and his angels, And prevailed not; neither was their place found any more in heaven. And the great dragon was cast out, that old serpent, called the Devil, and Satan, which deceiveth the whole world: he was cast out into the earth, and his angels were cast out with him. **And I heard a loud voice saying in heaven, Now is come salvation, and strength, and the kingdom of our God, and the power of his Christ: for the accuser of our brethren is cast down, which accused them before our God day and night.** *And they overcame him by the blood of the Lamb, and by the word of their testimony; and they loved not their lives unto the death.*   *Rev 12:7-11*

Those who have experienced war call it hell. Death, destruction, pain and suffering all bloom in the horrors of war. Even seemingly righteous causes dispense all too human agony. Can war in heaven be similar? How can angels suffer and die? How can they experience the pain of families separated or destroyed? How are heavenly places ruined? It is beyond comprehension in our earthly perspective; yet there is war in heaven, and it has to be horrible.

We know the outcome, but do we know the price? The price for salvation was the suffering and death of God's only Son, who overcame death in his victory. We don't know the pain of a heavenly war, but we do know the outcome. God is victorious and Satan's deception which originated our pain is cast out. No wonder the declaration of victory is proclaimed in a loud voice. What was done on earth will become a reality in heaven—and the result will surely be felt on earth. The joy of salvation will be restored in all its glory.

In the meantime we are accused in the earth and in heaven. The accusations are perpetual. I sleep, but my accuser does not. I can rest in the salvation of my God because he does not.

> *My help cometh from the LORD, which made heaven and earth.*
> *He will not suffer thy foot to be moved: he that keepeth thee will not slumber.*
> *Behold, he that keepeth Israel shall neither slumber nor sleep.*   *Ps 121:2-4*

I may rest but must not slumber through life. In the strength of the blood of Jesus Christ I can overcome. My testimony can be a picture that reflects the truth of his victory on earth and in heaven. An awareness of the accuser's work should keep me continuously sensitive to the danger of deception. The joy of victory in Christ should be a constant cause for rejoicing.

> *Arise, shine; for thy light is come, and the glory of the LORD is risen upon thee.*   *Isa 60:1*

Dear Lord Jesus:

My enemy has much of which to accuse me, but you have allowed me to enter your salvation. The accusations have no value even though they are true. The blood you shed is the only thing of value. My enemy may have deceived my ancestors in the garden, but God is not deceived. He knows a lie from the truth, even the truth of my broken state and its being covered with the truth of his love. Praise to my God who casts down the accuser and who allows me and his own to stand in his righteousness. I am lifted up but the accuser is cast down. Praise to you, Lord.

Lifted up in you

REFLECTION

There are accusers on the earth and an accuser in the heavenlies. It is "in earth, as it is in heaven" (Matt 6:10). In heaven, the accusation will be cast down. On the earth the effect of accusation is often destructive. Fault finding, lawsuits, complaining are all expressions of selfish accusations—the flesh. My God says be anxious for nothing. My God says be true to the truth. The accuser has no place in me, and my earthly accusers cannot crush my spirit. My spirit is alive because of God who is greater than any accuser. He has overcome and I overcome in him.

PRACTICE

The best defense against an accusation is truth. Ironically, in our case the truth is with our accuser. We are all sinners. The truth does not help; it condemns us. I am guilty and in my sin I am subject to judgment and the wrath of the God of truth. There must be another solution for me. There must be a defense for all of us who are conceived in sin.

The loud voice proclaims *now is come salvation*!

The eternal judge himself has become our salvation. He has become one of us in Jesus. He has become our savior in Christ. We can enter into salvation; and now truth becomes our salvation, because he is the truth.

Truth now exists in heaven and also in the earth. It is the truth of our guilt and the overcoming truth of his salvation. If we don't believe the truth of salvation, the world will tempt us to deny the truth of our guilt. The result is tragic.

123

For there are three that bear record in heaven, the Father, the Word, and the Holy Ghost: and these three are one. And there are three that bear witness in earth, the spirit, and the water, and the blood: and these three agree in one.
1 Jn 5:7-8

The blood of Christ covers our sin, and the water of the Word washes us so that we can walk in the purity of the Holy Spirit. All agree, and salvation has become truth in life. It is not just a hope or some obscure theology. It is imminently practical. In a particularly difficult time of life my pastor counseled me to be true to the truth. It was life-changing counsel. The power of truth contains both salvation and deliverance.

> Practice overcoming the accuser by knowing the truth, and letting the truth set you free. In fact, having escaped the criminal judgement of sin, you can overcome the accuser with aggressive action in the civil court of life. Speak of your deliverance. Speak of it in love, knowing the depth from which you have been rescued. In a previous exercise you were asked to write your testimony of salvation. Add to that writing a testimony of your deliverance.

28. Spiritual Warfare

And the dragon was wroth with the woman, and went to make war with the remnant of her seed, which keep the commandments of God, and have the testimony of Jesus Christ.   Rev 12:17

CONTEXT

*Therefore rejoice, ye heavens, and ye that dwell in them. Woe to the inhabiters of the earth and of the sea! for the devil is come down unto you, having great wrath, because he knoweth that he hath but a short time. And when the dragon saw that he was cast unto the earth, he persecuted the woman which brought forth the man child. And to the woman were given two wings of a great eagle, that she might fly into the wilderness, into her place, where she is nourished for a time, and times, and half a time, from the face of the serpent. And the serpent cast out of his mouth water as a flood after the woman, that he might cause her to be carried away of the flood. And the earth helped the woman, and the earth opened her mouth, and swallowed up the flood which the dragon cast out of his mouth. **And the dragon was wroth with the woman, and went to make war with the remnant of her seed, which keep the commandments of God, and have the testimony of Jesus Christ.** Rev 12:12-17*

One thing we can count on is this: the enemy of our soul hates us. The heavens may rejoice, being rid of the devil; their rejoicing will become a reality for the earth one day. In the meantime, our prayer continues to be *thy will be done on earth as it is in heaven.* There is much persecution of righteousness in the world today. The Word of God and even the existence of Christ is brought into question.

Jesus asked his disciples, *Whom do people say that I am* (Luke 9:18-21)? The response of the world today would be different—he is irrelevant. Spiritual warfare may well be avoided by minimizing Jesus in the world today. Unfortunately, the wrath of God may await those who continue in this irrational denial. The second question is more relevant—*Whom do you say that I am?* Now the issue is personal. If the answer is "the Christ of God," then I am accountable to live in the commandments of God and his testimony. Now I am subject to the wrath of Satan but gloriously under the protection of God. The enemy of my soul may come in like a flood, but I can flee into the protection of the God who loves me and has given himself for my protection. The body of Christ is truly a remnant; but it is a remnant kept by the living God.

Dear Lord Jesus:

What a precious remnant this is, Lord. A remnant made of those who live by the covenants of God and also live in your testimony, which is the fulness of that covenant. I am adopted, grafted in. The Jews are natural branches, broken off for my sake, but able to bring forth fruits of righteousness. I can bring fruits of righteousness because of the Holy Spirit. How rich the fullness can be when I grow in the grace of God's heritage on earth and in the fullness of your salvation.

Keeping believing.

REFLECTION

The enemy of God is also the enemy of my soul. The war in the heavenlies is in my soul as well. The Holy Spirit is in me and I am lifted up to the heavenlies. Satan is cast down and I am lifted up. No wonder there is such a contradiction in me. Praise to God, I know who wins in the heavenlies and I know who wins in me. In the meantime I will struggle, but stand in faith, hope and love.

They remain, they abide, and in them I find strength, and become established and settled in Christ.

PRACTICE

There are two attributes of the remnant, keeping the commandments of God, and having the testimony of Jesus Christ. There are two conditions of the remnant, spiritual warfare and the security of our place in Christ. As a part of the body of Christ we are safe, but as the remnant on this earth we are at war. It is a terrible war, one rooted in the wrath of a defeated enemy of God. The war has many fronts. Its worldly expression is found in humanism, sensualism, spiritism and legalism. Our calling as the remnant is to stand against those things which would destroy our heritage in God. God's promise is to protect and to do battle in our place.

> ... *When the enemy shall come in like a flood, the Spirit of the LORD shall lift up a standard against him. Isa 59:19*

The war may be in the earth, but there is a battle in our own soul. The enemy's purpose in our own life is to distract us from keeping commandments of God and to destroy our testimony of Jesus Christ. Our calling is to vigilantly recognize we are being attacked in the very identity we have as a part of the remnant. Our commission is to actively resist the enemy of our soul.

> *Be sober, be vigilant; because your adversary the devil, as a roaring lion, walketh about, seeking whom he may devour: Whom resist stedfast in the faith, knowing that the same afflictions are accomplished in your brethren that are in the world.* 1 Pet 5:8-9

If we humbly submit to God and resist the enemy, then our enemy will flee (James 4:7). To deny that there is a spiritual war or to do battle in our own strength is a guarantee of both frustration and failure. The battle may be the Lord's, but we have an active role in it. Our role is to keep the commandments of God and the testimony of Jesus Christ. The practice of spiritual warfare, however, is in humility and submission. Submission may be abstract with respect to God, but he has given us one another to practice submission.

> *Yea, all of you be subject one to another, and be clothed with humility: for God resisteth the proud, and giveth grace to the humble.*   *1 Pet 5:5*

Remember, the tribulation of spiritual warfare is common to us all. Practice spiritual warfare, serve the body of Christ. Set aside your own agenda for a day and look to the best interest of another person.

---

29. Hearing Ears

If any man have an ear, let him hear. ... Here is the patience
and the faith of the saints.   Rev 13:9-10b

CONTEXT

*And I stood upon the sand of the sea, and saw a beast rise
up out of the sea, having seven heads and ten horns, and
upon his horns ten crowns, and upon his heads the name
of blasphemy. And the beast which I saw was like unto a
leopard, and his feet were as the feet of a bear, and his
mouth as the mouth of a lion: and the dragon gave him his
power, and his seat, and great authority. And I saw one of
his heads as it were wounded to death; and his deadly
wound was healed: and all the world wondered after the
beast. And they worshipped the dragon which gave power
unto the beast: and they worshipped the beast, saying, Who
is like unto the beast? who is able to make war with him?
And there was given unto him a mouth speaking great things
and blasphemies; and power was given unto him to continue forty and two months. And he opened his mouth in
blasphemy against God, to blaspheme his name, and his
tabernacle, and them that dwell in heaven. And it was
given unto him to make war with the saints, and to overcome them: and power was given him over all kindreds,
and tongues, and nations. And all that dwell upon the
earth shall worship him, whose names are not written in
the book of life of the Lamb slain from the foundation of
the world. **If any man have an ear, let him hear.** He that
leadeth into captivity shall go into captivity: he that killeth
with the sword must be killed with the sword. **Here is the
patience and the faith of the saints.**   Rev 13:1-10*

No matter how sin is described, it is monstrous. All sin is blasphemy and the monster behind it all is the original blasphemer—Satan. There is an air of power behind the monster but it is only the power to deceive and destroy. One potent deception is the monster of sin is beautiful and irresistible, even worthy of worship. Amazing powers are attributed to wizardry and witchcraft; but like an illusionist, it's all a deception.

Sin is a powerful deception, one to be exposed by the Holy Spirit. Even Paul found the power of sin to be strong proclaiming, *O wretched man that I am! who shall deliver me from the body of this death* (Rom 7:24)? Like Paul, we all must find our deliverance only in the Lord Jesus Christ.

In time, the fullness of deception will be revealed as blasphemy. The words of the enemy are all hatred and blasphemy toward God and all of his creation. The blessing is, Satan's time to deceive and blaspheme is finite. God is eternal, and he has given eternal life to those of us who believe unto salvation. We are not only protected from the death of sinful blasphemy, we are preserved eternally. We struggle through this life in faith and the firm hope of God's eternal victory. The result is patience, the kind of patience that becomes love.

It is not so with those who are deceived and choose to not believe the truth. The deception becomes reality as the very acts of sin become the judgement of sin. Those who are snares to others will become snared, and the violent will experience the edge of violence. How much richer it is to hear the word of faith and then believe it in faith.

Dear Lord Jesus:

These are mysterious words, Lord, and yet you say we can hear and even understand. I know the world system has power, and I know it can easily overcome even those who are yours. The hearing of these words is painful, but understanding brings patience and faith. Lord, these are gifts of the Holy Spirit—that Spirit which seals me and lets your patience and faith live in me. The world and the flesh may overcome, but you overcame it all. I can live in the hope of that truth and with the patience of the Holy Spirit who sees past what is apparent.

Victory in you.

REFLECTION

Remembering faith and patience is a choice. Remembering, however, is not just idle thought. Idle thoughts are as destructive as idleness. Work is discipline, and the work of my mind is also discipline. I choose to think on the things of my God who has given me the gift of the Holy Spirit as a helper. The Holy Spirit speaks of the things of God. I can listen and apply his truth. I have ears to hear and can choose which way they are tuned. My flesh has a strong voice, one that is easy to hear but does not speak of faith and patience. I choose the voice of his spirit in my spirit. He is truth.

PRACTICE

One of the common phrases in scripture are the words of Jesus, "Who hath ears to hear, let him hear." His words compel us to go beyond words to gain understanding. Even this book of Revelation is introduced with a blessing for those who read, hear and keep. There is clearly more to hearing than to just hear.

The world hears the sound of salvation; but the noise of daily living drowns it out.

> *For this people's heart is waxed gross, and their ears are dull of hearing, and their eyes they have closed; lest at any time they should see with their eyes, and hear with their ears, and should understand with their heart, and should be converted, and I should heal them. But blessed are your eyes, for they see: and your ears, for they hear.*
> *Matt 13:15-16*

It is possible to hear and to believe unto salvation. Then we are truly blessed because the Holy Spirit will enrich our lives with understanding. Words of faith can become words of life as we choose to obey. In the roaring of my flesh and in the clamor of the world's strife I can hear the comfort of Jesus. As I learn to listen, I learn to obey, and the distractions fade away. Like the darkness dispels before the light, so also does the clamor flee before the peace of my God.

The first Rule of Saint Benedict begins with, "Listen carefully, my children, to the master's instructions, and attend to them with the ear of your heart."

Practice to hear by stopping to listen. Learn to hear the voice of God in daily life. It is more than stopping to smell the roses; it is letting the words of God become life, but it begins with listening. Mark your daily calendar with the word LIS-TEN and stop three times a day to do just that. It is amazing what listening will do for your hearing.

---

30. Applying Wisdom

> Here is wisdom. Let him that hath understanding ...
>
> Rev 13:18a

CONTEXT

> *And I beheld another beast coming up out of the earth;
> and he had two horns like a lamb, and he spake as a dragon.
> And he exerciseth all the power of the first beast before
> him, and causeth the earth and them which dwell therein
> to worship the first beast, whose deadly wound was healed.
> And he doeth great wonders, so that he maketh fire come
> down from heaven on the earth in the sight of men, And
> deceiveth them that dwell on the earth by the means of
> those miracles which he had power to do in the sight of the
> beast; saying to them that dwell on the earth, that they
> should make an image to the beast, which had the wound
> by a sword, and did live. And he had power to give life
> unto the image of the beast, that the image of the beast
> should both speak, and cause that as many as would not
> worship the image of the beast should be killed. And he
> causeth all, both small and great, rich and poor, free and
> bond, to receive a mark in their right hand, or in their
> foreheads: And that no man might buy or sell, save he that
> had the mark, or the name of the beast, or the number of
> his name. **Here is wisdom. Let him that hath understand-
> ing** count the number of the beast: for it is the number of a
> man; and his number is Six hundred threescore and six.*
>
> *Rev 13:11-18*

Sin is monstrous, but acceptance and promotion of sin is just
as heinous. In fact, covering and promoting sin is the first danger.
If we were to face sin directly we would surely reject it, seeing it

for what it is. Rather, the enemy of God, and our soul, prefers to be promoted in innocent, but powerful ways.

The world sought signs when Jesus walked the earth and that mind-set still exists. The enemy is a deceiver, and many are deceived into occult practices which promise power in and over life. The seeking of signs and spiritual powers fuels the new age religions, but a step is required before deception will draw men into the occult. That step is to cover up sin and erase the pain of our corporate and individual guilt.

How can there be sin, a transgression of the law of God, if there are no absolutes? There is great freedom in relativism. Truth is what I decide it is. What freedom—as the conviction of guilt is released I run freely into the snare of sin.

God says there is wisdom based on the understanding of truth. God says we are free, not to sin, but from its slavery. God says we are free to choose life.

> *Stand fast therefore in the liberty wherewith Christ hath made us free, and be not entangled again with the yoke of bondage.* Gal 5:1

Wisdom cries out and understanding speaks loudly (Prov 8:1). It takes real effort to deny the truth, but *Happy is the man that findeth wisdom, and the man that getteth understanding* (Prov 3:13). Flee deception-know truth and find liberty that cannot be turned to bondage.

Dear Lord Jesus:

An ear to hear and wisdom are a great gift, Lord. I pray I can hear what the Spirit says and have the wisdom to know its application. Praise to you, Lord, for your Word speaks truth and wisdom is for the asking. I thank you, Lord, for any wisdom that has come from the application of your Word in my life and in my relationships to my family, the world and to your body. It is a precious gift, Lord, but it is surely a treasure in an earthen vessel. Help me,

Lord, to have faith and to have patience. Help me, Lord, to prepare by study and developing skills of imparting your words in life. Thank you, Lord, for making it all possible. Thank you, Lord, for those who encourage me in your Word.

Thankful.

REFLECTION

The Lord is good, in his Word is knowledge; and it is truth. It is so contrary to the world it seems foolish. In reality the world is foolish because its knowledge has no basis in truth. It is just a semi-true story. Without truth understanding becomes relative. Understanding becomes what my flesh wants it to be. What then of wisdom? In the flesh it becomes destruction; it is division. In the Spirit it is life and it is unity. What then of diversity? How wonderful our Lord is; how diverse and yet one in truth. Praise to him who brings diversity together in truth.

PRACTICE

Life is not just a game of trivial pursuit—an aggregation of random facts. No, the process is to learn and understand the implications of what is learned. Still, wisdom is more than understanding; it is giving understanding life. In the words of Jesus: "If ye know these things, happy are ye if ye do them" (John 13:17). Wisdom is based on truth, and we can find truth in the Lord himself. Its reflection is often contrary to what would be expected in worldly eyes.

> *Who is a wise man and endued with knowledge among you? let him shew out of a good conversation his works with meekness of wisdom. But if ye have bitter envying and strife in your hearts, glory not, and lie not against the truth. This wisdom descendeth not from above, but is earthly, sensual, devilish. For where envying and strife is,*

there is confusion and every evil work. But the wisdom
that is from above is first pure, then peaceable, gentle, and
easy to be intreated, full of mercy and good fruits, without
partiality, and without hypocrisy. And the fruit of righ-
teousness is sown in peace of them that make peace.

James 3:13-18

Practice applying wisdom. Decide that the Word of God is true, and let the Holy Spirit bear fruits of righteousness in your life. Pray for the Lord's conviction when anger, bitterness and strife threaten to steal the fruit of wisdom. Be quick to recognize the wisdom of the world. Be a minister of peace in your own life, then the ministry of peace will be an expression of wisdom applied. Today, decide to speak words of comfort in every place you venture.

31. Redemption's Song

And they sung as it were a new song before the throne, and before the four beasts, and the elders: and no man could learn that song but the hundred and forty and four thousand, which were redeemed from the earth.   Rev 14:3

CONTEXT

And I looked, and, lo, a Lamb stood on the mount Sion, and with him an hundred forty and four thousand, having his Father's name written in their foreheads. And I heard a voice from heaven, as the voice of many waters, and as the voice of a great thunder: and I heard the voice of harpers harping with their harps: **And they sung as it were a new song before the throne, and before the four beasts, and the elders: and no man could learn that song but the hundred and forty and four thousand, which were redeemed from the earth.** *These are they which were not defiled with women; for they are virgins. These are they which follow the Lamb whithersoever he goeth. These were redeemed from among men, being the firstfruits unto God and to the Lamb. And in their mouth was found no guile: for they are without fault before the throne of God.*

Rev 14:1-5

The Lamb King might make a good movie title. The psalmist declares that the Lord will, *set my king upon my holy hill of Zion* (Ps 2:6). The King is a lamb, sacrificed for the sins of the world so that he might truly rule in righteousness. The lamb of God was sacrificed alone, even forsaken, but in his holy hill he is not alone. The overcoming Lamb King is accompanied by thousands who belong to God. The voices of heaven are not silent and there is a mountain filled with rejoicing and music.

There is a new song, a special song, one reserved for the redeemed. Who can know the grace of salvation except those who have received it? It is said to sing the blues you must have experienced great loss and sadness. So also with the song of redemption; it is a living song, one that expresses and rejoices in life with the Savior.

People have speculated on what could be accomplished for the kingdom of God if just one person were totally sold out to the purposes, plans and pleasures of God. Extend that speculation to thousands of followers all serving in holiness because of Christ. It is no wonder that they follow the Lamb where ever he went, he is the source of their living song.

Dear Lord Jesus:

Praise you Lord for redemption. Praise you for a new song which is the joy of my salvation. What a precious gift you have given us Lord. What a treasure we have to sing about. No song in heaven or earth is greater than the song of the new covenant, which is made in your own blood. Praise to you Lord, for the gift of a song to praise you with. With your song we can strengthen and edify one another; we can also proclaim your salvation to the world. Lord, teach me to sing it with zeal. Teach me to sing it with truth and with conviction. Teach me to sing it without ceasing.

Singing joy.

REFLECTION

"The Joy of the Lord is my strength," that is a new song because he has promised and is becoming my strength. His song is the song of redemption. His song is the song of salvation. His song is the song of restoration. I can hear the music, I can respond to the song. I can sing the song with my God and with those who enter into his salvation. Praise to my God who sings from the pain of his own submission; who sings the glory of resurrection. Praise to my God who sings songs of love to me. Praise to my God who strengthens me with his love, to walk in this weary world.

PRACTICE:

One of the pleasant things to do on this earth is to climb a hill or a mountain and just enjoy the view. The view can be inspiring and restful. From the top of a hill all of our perspective changes. We can see where we are, and even where we have been. The elevation lets us put problems in perspective as well. With a little imagination, everything of this world can seem smaller. From the hill, you can even sing a song of praise for the creation of God and the beauty of his world.

From the hilltop you might see pollution or destruction and sadness fills your heart. The view from mount Zion is the same. It reveals the pollution of sin in the creation of God. The perspective is different however, because the hill is meant to be seen from *the valley of the shadow of death* (Ps 23:4).

> *Ye are the light of the world. A city that is set on an hill cannot be hid. Neither do men light a candle, and put it under a bushel, but on a candlestick; and it giveth light unto all that are in the house. Let your light so shine before men, that they may see your good works, and glorify your Father which is in heaven.* Matt 5:14-16

In the living of my life, and likely yours, it is too late to be found without fault. Somehow, I find myself on that hill with a song in my heart, the song of the redeemed. The lamb has made me holy in his own blood. I am redeemed and can sing the new song. When the new song fills my mouth there is no room for guile. When I follow the Lamb there is no place for fault to be found. When I live on his hill, the light of his life will shine forth.

Resolve to live as if everyone can see your light and in seeing it they will see the light of your Savior. The darkness may be a good place to hide, but we are in, and of, the light—his light.

Then spake Jesus again unto them, saying, I am the light of the world: he that followeth me shall not walk in darkness, but shall have the light of life.   *John 8:12*

Practice hilltop living by taking a trip to the highest place in your town. Look around. Rejoice in the beauty and weep over the destruction you see. Go back at night. See how the darkness has covered the unsightly areas. Only the lights can be seen and on a clear night the lights of heaven and earth can almost become intermingled.

32. Patient Faith

Here is the patience of the saints: here are they that keep the commandments of God, and the faith of Jesus.

Rev 14:12

CONTEXT

*And I saw another angel fly in the midst of heaven, having the everlasting gospel to preach unto them that dwell on the earth, and to every nation, and kindred, and tongue, and people, Saying with a loud voice, Fear God, and give glory to him; for the hour of his judgment is come: and worship him that made heaven, and earth, and the sea, and the fountains of waters. And there followed another angel, saying, Babylon is fallen, is fallen, that great city, because she made all nations drink of the wine of the wrath of her fornication. And the third angel followed them, saying with a loud voice, If any man worship the beast and his image, and receive his mark in his forehead, or in his hand, The same shall drink of the wine of the wrath of God, which is poured out without mixture into the cup of his indignation; and he shall be tormented with fire and brimstone in the presence of the holy angels, and in the presence of the Lamb: And the smoke of their torment ascendeth up for ever and ever: and they have no rest day nor night, who worship the beast and his image, and whosoever receiveth the mark of his name. **Here is the patience of the saints: here are they that keep the commandments of God, and the faith of Jesus.** And I heard a voice from heaven saying unto me, Write, Blessed are the dead which die in the Lord from henceforth: Yea, saith the Spirit, that they may rest from their labours; and their works do follow them.*

Rev 14:6-13

The good news of our God is an everlasting gospel. It is a rich gospel, one that should be loudly proclaimed to everyone that dwells on the earth. We know we are sinners even if we will not admit it. Admitting our sinful nature would compel us to either fear God or deny his existence. The fear of God evokes worship and enables the grace of an everlasting gospel. The time is at hand, if not for the world, for us individually. Our choice is to worship the God who created all things including the everlasting gospel.

Somehow, the world does not mind the gospel being preached, even loudly. It can be ignored or drowned in the cares of life. What the world cannot tolerate is the announcement of judgement. Who can judge another's choice of lifestyle or right to make living choices? To proclaim judgement is to imply the existence of absolutes involving right and wrong. "Every enlightened person knows truth is relative," says the world. Still the Word of God and its announcement of judgement is unsettling, even to the enlightened. There is no rest day nor night for those who are deceived in the world's enlightenment.

How patient we must be, who believe the gospel. God does not desire any to perish in the judgement of sin. Our lives of faith and obedience are the testimonies of his grace and even in death, our works follow us. It has always been so. The works of Moses, the patriarchs, prophets apostles, and followers of Christ are such loud voices that they are still heard today. Even modern men of God enter their rest, leaving ministries with everlasting impact on the earth. What a marvelous heritage we have in Christ and in the body of Christ which enable his works of salvation to follow even into eternity.

Dear Lord Jesus:

Praise to my God who is to be feared and who is love. Your wrath is terrible indeed, but love is your very nature. You love your creation and want none to perish. God's love is so great he gave you, his only son, so that we may discover its richness. God's wrath is terrible but it is reserved for those who choose to reject his great salvation. Your faith is my salvation and the keeping of your way is my blessing. Your wrath is destructive, but your chastening is deliverance. I must never confuse the two. I live in your love. Even hard things are expressions of your love for me. I may not understand fully, but I know the depth of my flesh and also the depth of your love.

Thank you.

REFLECTION

The commandment of God is to love him, myself and others. The faith of Jesus is to love and know this love will draw others to him. I love my family and have faith in his love to draw them to himself. It is his love I can express to them so restoration and life can be discovered and renewed. The Lord will draw those who are to be saved. My job is to love and to share the source of love—my God who has made himself real in his only son, my savior, Jesus Christ. He is Lord and has overcome the death of sin. I owe it all to him. Love and faith give me hope.

PRACTICE

One humorous reflection often quipped about scripture, is the warning not to pray for patience because tribulation is what works patience into our lives (Rom 5:3). I rebel at that thought, even in its element of truth. I know we should pray for patience, it is one of the qualities of God we should desire. I think it is in not praying for patience and seeking the ways of God in our life we risk tribulation. Patience through tribulation may very well be the default way to receive this marvelous grace.

The patience of a living saint is found in faith and obedience. The choice to obey the Word of God surely requires the grace of patience. In our flesh, the things of God are hard and often don't seem to make sense, especially in this hurry-up world. One of the most difficult words to hear is wait.

There is a promise of renewed strength in waiting on God (Is 40:31), but waiting without prayer may be fruitless. Someone said fasting without prayer is just dieting, in like manner the work of patient faith may be lost in just idle waiting. Instead, pray with the psalmist:

> *Shew me thy ways, O LORD; teach me thy paths.*
> *Lead me in thy truth, and teach me: for thou art the God of*
> *my salvation; on thee do I wait all the day.*   *Ps 25:1-5*

Practice patient faith by resting in the confidence of God's commitment to work his grace into your life. Pray boldly for patience and then *let patience have her perfect work, that ye may be perfect and entire, wanting nothing* (James 1:4).

---

33. Harvest Time

> And another angel came out of the temple, crying with a
> loud voice to him that sat on the cloud, Thrust in thy sickle,
> and reap: for the time is come for thee to reap; for the
> harvest of the earth is ripe.   Rev 14:15

CONTEXT

*And I looked, and behold a white cloud, and upon the cloud
one sat like unto the Son of man, having on his head a
golden crown, and in his hand a sharp sickle.* **And another angel came out of the temple, crying with a loud
voice to him that sat on the cloud, Thrust in thy sickle,
and reap: for the time is come for thee to reap; for the
harvest of the earth is ripe.** *And he that sat on the cloud
thrust in his sickle on the earth; and the earth was reaped.
And another angel came out of the temple which is in
heaven, he also having a sharp sickle. And another angel
came out from the altar, which had power over fire; and
cried with a loud cry to him that had the sharp sickle, saying, Thrust in thy sharp sickle, and gather the clusters of
the vine of the earth; for her grapes are fully ripe. And the
angel thrust in his sickle into the earth, and gathered the
vine of the earth, and cast it into the great winepress of the
wrath of God. And the winepress was trodden without the
city, and blood came out of the winepress, even unto the
horse bridles, by the space of a thousand and six hundred
furlongs.*   *Rev 14:14-20*

It's popular today for film makers to make war movies which
vividly display the horrors of war. Although there may be some
sense of heroics and even victory, mercy and grace are lost in the
blood of sacrifice and death.

One of the truly destructive conflicts in our history was the American Civil War. Out of that struggle came a hymn that could only be written by experiencing the horrors of war. The Battle Hymn of the Republic refrains with glory and hallelujah's but its verses speak of the vintage of God's wrath.

> *Mine eyes have seen the glory of the coming of the Lord;*
> *He is trampling out the vintage where the grapes of wrath are stored;*
> *He hath loosed the fateful lightening of his terrible swift sword;*
> *His truth is marching on.*

There is a harvest, and it's the Lord's harvest. It is he who wears the crown of glory, and his sharp sickle reaps the harvest of the earth. Oh, to be a part of that harvest. Oh, to see the sharp Word of God penetrate and bring forth repentance unto salvation.

A harvest, yes, but also a vintage of God's wrath. It is not our Savior, but an angel of God's wrath that wields this sharp instrument; and the harvest is to experience the wrath of the living God. The song of battle, as horrible as it appears, is only a shadow of the press of God's wrath.

The mercy of Christ's sharp sickle may seem painful but the refrain is *Glory! Glory! Hallelujah!*

To miss the grace of his mercy leaves *a certain fearful looking for of judgment and fiery indignation, which shall devour the adversaries* (Heb 10:27). There is no glory in that place for *it is a fearful thing to fall into the hands of the living God* (Heb 10:31).

Today is the day of salvation—*Our God is marching on.*

Dear Lord Jesus:

Is it time to reap, Lord? It seems like wheat and tares are so fully grown togther that reaping will be difficult. Yet, Lord, you know the time; and you know how to reap an individual life. Thank you, Lord, for finding me and for drawing me to yourself. What of reaping, Lord? Am I a sharp sickle to be used in the harvest? Is it your work and I am only to be available, and to love with your love? How marvelous is your love, Lord. I want to see others drawn to you, yet I constrain the confrontation of your sharp edge. Help me to know when to wait, when to water and when to harvest.

Loving in you.

REFLECTION

Times come, opportunities come, problems come—it's just life. They come and they go as life moves on. There is a critical time however, it is a time of harvest. There will soon be a great harvest, but for now there is a time in individual lives which must confront eternity. God knows who will be saved; I do not. My job is to love with his love. My job is to love God and let him love others through me. How do I confront a person in error? How do I confront a person in deception? How do I avoid error and deception myself? The fear of God and the love of God keep me in his word and keep me seeking his ways. How can I share the strength of this place with others?

PRACTICE

One of the wonderful aspects of the earth are its seasons. There is a time to plant, a time to water, a time to harvest and a time to rest. The apostle Paul speaks of planting and watering but says it is God that gives the increase (1 Cor 3:7). As a very amateur gardener I know just how true this principle is. Even with careful planting and watering, what comes out of the earth is always a miracle of the grace of God to me. Even with a sparse harvest I continue to labor, finding joy in the effort as well as the reward.

The harvest of souls for the kingdom of God is even more mysterious and is rooted in compassion as well as the work of planting and watering. Jesus saw harvest time in the pain and suffering of the world.

But when he saw the multitudes, he was moved with compassion on them, because they fainted, and were scattered abroad, as sheep having no shepherd. Then saith he unto his disciples, The harvest truly is plenteous, but the labourers are few; Pray ye therefore the Lord of the harvest, that he will send forth labourers into his harvest.

Matt 9:36-38

Jesus could look on the multitude and see their broken hope and pain. He said pray for laborers—individuals. As a laborer responding to this prayer, my calling is to individuals. My compassion is for a hurting person. My ministry is to nourish and water individual souls.

> Practice your calling as a laborer in the harvest. Be vulnerable; open your heart to someone in your life. Water with the water that has refreshed your own life.

34. Seeing Holiness

> Who shall not fear thee, O Lord, and glorify thy name? for
> thou only art holy: ...   Rev 15:4a

CONTEXT

> *And I saw another sign in heaven, great and marvellous,*
> *seven angels having the seven last plagues; for in them is*
> *filled up the wrath of God. And I saw as it were a sea of*
> *glass mingled with fire: and them that had gotten the vic-*
> *tory over the beast, and over his image, and over his mark,*
> *and over the number of his name, stand on the sea of glass,*
> *having the harps of God. And they sing the song of Moses*
> *the servant of God, and the song of the Lamb, saying, Great*
> *and marvellous are thy works, Lord God Almighty; just*
> *and true are thy ways, thou King of saints.* ***Who shall not***
> ***fear thee, O Lord, and glorify thy name? for thou only***
> ***art holy:*** *for all nations shall come and worship before*
> *thee; for thy judgments are made manifest.*   *Rev 15:1-4*

One of the hardest concepts to grasp in Scripture is the wrath
of God, and yet it is called great and marvelous. The physical
manifestations of his wrath are truly great. They are called plagues,
something which is overwhelming and impossible to resist. They
are marvelous in the sense that we cannot comprehend the magnitude of their terror. Still, we shall witness his wrath and rejoice in
our redemption. It is a joy today to know that God's wrath is not
reserved for us as believers. We shall stand and sing the song of
Moses, the song of our passage from death to life and of the victory of our God over evil. It is a long song but opens with these
words:

> *Then sang Moses and the children of Israel this song unto*
> *the LORD, and spake, saying, I will sing unto the LORD,*

149

for he hath triumphed gloriously: the horse and his rider hath he thrown into the sea. The LORD is my strength and song, and he is become my salvation: he is my God, and I will prepare him an habitation; my father's God, and I will exalt him. The LORD is a man of war: the LORD is his name. Exod 15:1-3

The song of Moses becomes the song of the Lamb when it is applied to our own heart. The song of the Lamb is a personal song; a song of redemption in our own life. It is meant to be sung in eternity; but it is being composed today, in our own life.

The psalmist points out, "God made known his ways to Moses and his works to the children of Israel" (Ps 103:7). What a difference it makes! The children of Israel walked paths of repeated rebellion and repentance. Moses walked in the knowledge of God's ways. In eternity his works and his ways come together. We can celebrate both today. He lives in our circumstance and in our heart.

Who shall not fear God? Ultimately all will come to fear him; but the form of that fear will be quite different for those who are his and for those who are subject to his wrath. For one it shall be terror, but for his own it shall be an expression of his love. It is more than awe and respect; it is a deep sense of knowing what we deserve and what his grace has provided for us. It will draw us to him. It will cause us to seek his ways as well as his mighty works. It is for today as well as eternity.

Dear Lord Jesus:

The song of an overcomer is a song of fear and of glory. You are holy, and any holiness I have is in, and because of, you, Lord. I know a little of myself and fear you because of what I know. I cannot face the depth and horror of sin, but you did, Lord. You carried the fullness of its horror and overcame. If I overcome, it is in your strength, your fear, and your glory. I have proven my inability, and in it I have experienced your great ability. Thank you, Lord, for fear and for love. Thank you, Lord, for a taste of the horror of sin so that I may know the cost of my redemption. You are the Lord; you are holy. I am blessed and in it show the glory of your name.

Purchased in blood.

REFLECTION

It takes arrogance not to fear God, and it leads to rebellion. The Psalmist describes the arrogance of the wicked, saying "there is no fear of God before their eyes" (Ps 36:1). Satan's rebellion was rooted in arrogance and the lack of holy fear. He was deceived, and practices deception. He is called the father of lies. What a comfort the fear of God is. When I face up to the truth of my deception, my sin, then I fear God and receive his love and his salvation. The fear of God becomes the love of God which keeps me and restores me to his grace. To deny the fear is to deny his love; it is to say who needs it. What arrogance!

PRACTICE

One of the most common concepts in scripture is the fear of God. Over 500 verses mention the theme and many other passages demonstrate its effect. It is a new testament principle as well as an old testament example. Unfortunately, it is a principle that is virtually ignored in the church and its teachings today. When it is taught it is relegated to something like awe or respect.

It is pretty hard to read about the wrath of God and his terrible judgments without dealing with the fear of God. Fear surely has an element of terror, but it also has an element of confidence. God has shown us the horrible consequences of sin in his Word; and realizing the immediate and eternal effect of sin should truly cause us to fear. It should cause us to run to his salvation.

We are all promised judgment, and for some it will be his wrath. For those who fear him and turn to his grace and mercy, it will be a point of rejoicing. Some believers fear the judgment of Christ, but in it is the promise of our dead works being consumed in its fire. I will be glad to be relieved of that burden, for then I can see him as he is.

I wonder what emotions I will have as a spectator to his wrath. I know what emotions I should have today; a powerful desire to see others escape wrath and enter the grace of his judgement. That is where practicing the fear of God finds its expression. The fear of God is not something to do; rather, it is something to be. It is, however, rooted in our testimony of his grace in our life.

> In a previous meditation you were asked to write the testimony of your salvation. Now write the testimony of your obedience. Somehow the words *go and sin no more* must echo in our lives. Let the fear of God keep you from sin and the love of God hold you in his grace.

35. Untouchable Glory

> And the temple was filled with smoke from the glory of
> God, and from his power; and no man was able to enter
> into the temple, ...   Rev 15:8a

CONTEXT

> *And after that I looked, and, behold, the temple of the tab-*
> *ernacle of the testimony in heaven was opened: And the*
> *seven angels came out of the temple, having the seven*
> *plagues, clothed in pure and white linen, and having their*
> *breasts girded with golden girdles. And one of the four*
> *beasts gave unto the seven angels seven golden vials full*
> *of the wrath of God, who liveth for ever and ever.* **And the**
> **temple was filled with smoke from the glory of God, and**
> **from his power; and no man was able to enter into the**
> **temple,** *till the seven plagues of the seven angels were ful-*
> *filled.*   Rev 15:5-8

The temple on earth was a tabernacle of the testimony of God's
presence. The reality in heaven is a testimony as well. It's a testimony of his glory; it's revelation of his power. Both faces of his
glory and power are shown: the power of his salvation and of his
wrath.

God's wrath is delivered by angels who are clothed much like
the priests of the old testament whose role was to minister to God
on behalf of the people and also to hear from God on their behalf.
Even in the last days, God's judgments are delivered through created beings—angels, but created just like us. The vials of the wrath
of God are actually from one of the four beasts which some inter-
pret to be people.

Can it be that we are creating our own wrath? As we entertain
evil, is not that very evil the seed of his wrath? If so, how can we
be so arrogant to blame God for the horrible consequences of sin in

the world today? Those who face the fullness of his wrath have no excuse—it is the essence of their own wickedness. Is there any other alternative but confession and repentance? Is there any hope, except in God and his provision through Christ Jesus?

The temple may be opened, but it is filled with smoke. The glory and power of God are a mystery, but Christ is its revelation. The temple is open because of Christ. His glory and power are mysterious, but we can enter in and experience their fulness. There will come a time when no man may enter because of his wrath, which once begun must be completed.

God doesn't start something without completing it, including the good work he is doing in our lives (Phil 1:6).

Dear Lord Jesus:

Your glory and your power are mysteries, Lord, especially when your wrath is being expressed. The world says, how can a God of love do harm? It is an excuse and not the truth. Your wrath is as real as your love, Lord. Praise to you for purity and for holiness. Only you are holy; and arrogance has no place in your temple. It has no place in me, and it has no place in the body of Christ. Chastening is good for me, it teaches me the fear of God and deals with my arrogance. Praise God, I am escaped from wrath because of salvation. Your wrath toward me becomes chastening; it's designed to draw me to your holiness, not to destroy me or keep me from you.

Chastened and turned.

REFLECTION

What error it is to picture a mushy, lovey-dovey God. He is a jealous God, one who executes his wrath on workers of iniquity. He is holy and his judgments are holy and pure. To those who receive his love, he chastens out of love. He loves all of his creation. He judges those who reject his love, and works in those who receive it. Even his chastening may seem harsh, but it is for good. He is perfect love. He is infinite in wisdom and sovereign in power. He loves me, knows what is good for me, and is in complete control. I can trust him in all things and at all times. What peace!

PRACTICE

The scripture calls us temples of God because the Spirit of God dwells in us (1 Cor 3:16). We can be open testimonies just like the temple of the heavenlies, but rather than wrath, our testimony should be of his grace and mercy. Jesus tells us to pray his will be done in earth as it is in heaven. There may be no better place to begin than to realize we are temples of God and the tabernacle of his testimony on earth.

We have the potential to judge, and we have the potential to bless. We have the power to hurt, and we have the power to heal. We have been given a testimony that can keep men from entering his glory or to invite them to experience it in this life, and for eternity. What a treasure God has put in this earthen vessel.

Can others see Jesus in our testimony? If they do see glory in us, do they turn to him or do they praise us for our goodness? The secret to being a faithful testimony is twofold: first, the testimony must be true, and secondly it should reflect the source, not the vessel. We can err in both elements.

To begin to practice being a true and living testimony, a dangerous prayer is necessary.

Search me, O God, and know my heart: try me, and know my thoughts:
And see if there be any wicked way in me, and lead me in the way everlasting.   *Ps 139:23-24*

God will honor this prayer, and our job is to respond by turning to him as the revelation of our wicked ways becomes apparent. The way everlasting is to testify of him in truth. Begin by searching out the qualities of his character and choosing to speak

155

to someone about that quality in your own life, being sure to say it is God's gift.

In previous meditations, the practice was to write a testimony of salvation and one of obedience. Remember, ultimately this is his testimony, not yours. It is not what God has done in you, but who God is in you. There is a difference. Now write a testimony of his praise. It may be appropriate to select an incident in your testimony to describe how his grace was worked out in your own life. Describe an attribute of the character of God which is unfolding in your own character.

36. Righteous Repentance

And I heard another out of the altar say, Even so, Lord God Almighty, true and righteous are thy judgments. ... and they repented not to give him glory.   Rev 16:7, 9b

CONTEXT

*And I heard a great voice out of the temple saying to the seven angels, Go your ways, and pour out the vials of the wrath of God upon the earth. And the first went, and poured out his vial upon the earth; and there fell a noisome and grievous sore upon the men which had the mark of the beast, and upon them which worshipped his image. And the second angel poured out his vial upon the sea; and it became as the blood of a dead man: and every living soul died in the sea. And the third angel poured out his vial upon the rivers and fountains of waters; and they became blood. And I heard the angel of the waters say, Thou art righteous, O Lord, which art, and wast, and shalt be, because thou hast judged thus. For they have shed the blood of saints and prophets, and thou hast given them blood to drink; for they are worthy. **And I heard another out of the altar say, Even so, Lord God Almighty, true and righteous are thy judgments.** And the fourth angel poured out his vial upon the sun; and power was given unto him to scorch men with fire. And men were scorched with great heat, and blasphemed the name of God, which hath power over these plagues: **and they repented not to give him glory.** And the fifth angel poured out his vial upon the seat of the beast; and his kingdom was full of darkness; and they gnawed their tongues for pain, And blasphemed the God of heaven because of their pains and their sores, and repented not of their deeds. And the sixth angel poured out his vial upon the great river Euphrates; and the water*

157

thereof was dried up, that the way of the kings of the east
might be prepared. And I saw three unclean spirits like
frogs come out of the mouth of the dragon, and out of the
mouth of the beast, and out of the mouth of the false prophet.
For they are the spirits of devils, working miracles, which
go forth unto the kings of the earth and of the whole world,
to gather them to the battle of that great day of God Al-
mighty.   *Rev 16:1-14*

The righteousness of God demands the horrors of sin be judged.
The entry of sin in the garden brought a curse upon the earth and
words of judgement on man. God is true to his word. Sin shall be
judged, and its own horrors have become the execution of judgement. The earth suffers today and man continues to pursue evil
ways even in the face of judgement.

Just how bad does it have to get for man to repent and cry out
to God for salvation? Apparently, man will continue in sin regardless of circumstance. Without repentance, the way of sin is to blame
God for the consequences of our own sinful way. What blasphemy
it is to sin; and then, in the face of a righteous God, blame him for
the pain that results.

How can anyone be saved from wrath? As Paul proclaimed:
"O wretched man that I am! who shall deliver me from the body of
this death" (Rom 7:24)? The answer is in—"But God!" It is by
the grace of God that we might believe the truth, repent and see
God as true and righteous. Then we can give him glory not only
for justice but for redeeming mercy.

Dear Lord Jesus:

You are true and righteous. Your judgements are true, and I
am surely worthy of judgement. You loved me even with me being
only worthy of judgement. You bore my judgement of death even
though you were worthy of glory. Praise you, Lord. Thank you,
Lord. When I consider my unworthiness and its depth, your salvation is unbelievable, but true. I choose to believe today, Lord. I

choose to repent today, Lord. Deception is irrational, Lord. It turns judgement into blame, so that you are blasphemed rather than glorified in repentance. Judgement is obvious, yet unseen in deception.

Thank you for clarity.

REFLECTION

When something goes wrong it is easy to blame God. How can God, who is love, allow or do such a thing? The complaint sounds a little like a teenager seeking to be like the world, but constrained by loving parents. Judgement is one way God calls us to repentance, and his wrath is the consequence of choosing not to repent. In repentance, we may also experience problems, but they are designed to teach the fear of God so that we can live in the love of God. God is worthy of glory; we are worthy of judgement. Somehow, in repentance, we change directions from his judgement to his glory.

PRACTICE

Somehow, as a Christian we must be able to get beyond circumstantial living. Jesus taught we really shouldn't be concerned with the struggles and cares of the world. Rather, we should seek the kingdom of God.

It sounds mystical to live beyond circumstance, especially when I wake every morning facing them. I live in a circumstantial world, surrounded by circumstantial people. The news and public voices, even clerical voices, seem to shout about circumstances. Political and moral issues all come together as we strive to find circumstantial solutions for the problems of life. Jesus says: "I have overcome the world" (John 16:33) and Scripture proclaims:

> *Blessed be God, even the Father of our Lord Jesus Christ, the Father of mercies, and the God of all comfort; Who*

comforteth us in all our tribulation, that we may be able to comfort them which are in any trouble, by the comfort wherewith we ourselves are comforted of God.

2 Cor 1:3-4

Righteous repentance may be found in just relaxing. Repentance means to turn around; go the other direction. Perhaps we can get beyond circumstantial living by comforting, or at least focusing on, someone else.

I think a picture of this grace is found in the spirit of a child. Children seem to be free of fretting over circumstances. Perhaps that is why Jesus encourages us to be like a little child in seeking his kingdom.

Practice repentance by being with a child today. Read a story to a child. There are plenty of opportunities for this to occur—nurseries, schools, hospitals, to name a few. Who knows, in blessing you my be blessed; and in comforting you may be comforted.

---

37. A Completed Work

> And the seventh angel poured out his vial into the air; and there came a great voice out of the temple of heaven, from the throne, saying, It is done. Rev 16:17

CONTEXT

> *Behold, I come as a thief. Blessed is he that watcheth, and keepeth his garments, lest he walk naked, and they see his shame. And he gathered them together into a place called in the Hebrew tongue Armageddon. **And the seventh angel poured out his vial into the air; and there came a great voice out of the temple of heaven, from the throne, saying, It is done.** And there were voices, and thunders, and lightnings; and there was a great earthquake, such as was not since men were upon the earth, so mighty an earthquake, and so great. And the great city was divided into three parts, and the cities of the nations fell: and great Babylon came in remembrance before God, to give unto her the cup of the wine of the fierceness of his wrath. And every island fled away, and the mountains were not found. And there fell upon men a great hail out of heaven, every stone about the weight of a talent: and men blasphemed God because of the plague of the hail; for the plague thereof was exceeding great. Rev 16:15-21*

Behold! It's not a word in common use today; and even its definition, "look and see," lacks fullness. It is used thousands of times in Scripture and always to describe an amazing sight or insight. God said of creation: "behold, it was very good" (Gen 1:31). Behold is the "Aha" word of meditation. It is much richer than look and see; it is to perceive the depth of all that is implied. It is the truth that sets us free. It is what we are seeking when we meditate on his Word.

161

Behold is also a response. It is a response to the Lord who always comes in surprising ways. He says that he comes as a thief—when we least expect it. When we see his hand in our life, it is usually a surprise, and we must respond with—behold.

Behold, his amazing work in our life. Behold, our readiness to praise and also obey. Our calling is to be ready, expecting a miracle, living ready to sing the song of beholding. Behold God is great! Behold I am ready!

The works of God seem continuous to us as we live our lives each day. Creation was also a process of several days, but there came a day when God rested. It was done, and he called it very good. The fierceness of his wrath has a completion as well. Sin was finished on the cross, and the power of finished sin will be broken in that day. Some may hate and blaspheme God in that day; but for us who believe, it will be—Behold, it is done!

Dear Lord Jesus:

You declared it is finished, and the wrath of which I am worthy was covered in your blood. God says it is done, and his wrath will be executed so that a new heaven and earth can be made. It is done, so that his body and his bride may become one. It is finished, it is done, in eternity they are the same. Praise you, Lord, for your work finished the sting of death and restoration is possible because *it is done*. In the meantime you are completing a good work in me and in your body. You are conforming us all to your image, making us ready for the bride.

Loved in you.

REFLECTION

It is done—what hopeful words these are for today. The words are an assurance of God's work and purpose which is to be completed. It is done, anchors my hope. It is finished, anchors my faith. Because of these anchors I live in love today. Praise to my

God who knows me and still loves me. He is working in me and will work in me as I open myself to let him do so. Some day I will hear, *it is done*, for now I live in *it is finished* and being done. He is faithful to save me; and he is faithful to restore me. He is the love I live in today.

PRACTICE

One of the most satisfying times of life is when something is finished. Whether it is building a house or just cleaning out the garage, getting it done brings a feeling of rest. It is the rest of God found in creation and completion.

The busy world wants to rob us of the satisfaction of completed work. It seems that nothing is ever finished. We start several projects at once and jump from project to project to the extent that we don't even notice when something is done. Even if we do, we question how well it was done. Our enemy has stolen the "Behold" from our lives; and in its place there is weariness, frustration and discouragement.

This Revelation opens with the revealed proclaiming himself:

> *I am Alpha and Omega, the beginning and the ending, saith the Lord, which is, and which was, and which is to come, the Almighty.*   *Rev 1:8*

There is nothing incomplete in Christ and there shall be nothing incomplete in each of us. Even for the haters of our God there is reserved an *it is done*. But for us, the promise is to be able to see him as he is, and to be changed into his very image.

> *And we know that all things work together for good to them that love God, to them who are the called according to his purpose. For whom he did foreknow, he also did predestinate to be conformed to the image of his Son, that he might be the firstborn among many brethren.*   *Rom 8:28-29*

It has been said that if you can understand, or behold, Romans 8:28, life would take on purpose and meaning. I think verse 29 may actually hold the key, for it is there the completed work is revealed. Oh! To be like Jesus, in this world and forever. What a destiny, what an assurance of *it is done*.

While we watch and wait for the fullness of his work, we can experience the rest and the joy of completing tasks today. The trick is to decide to notice when something is done. We need to quit focusing on the "to do" list and rejoice in the things that have been scratched off. Perhaps a "done" list is as important as a "to do" list.

> Practice living life as a completed work, stop after the next project, regardless of magnitude, and rest. Behold it as a job well done.

38. Called and Faithful

These shall make war with the Lamb, and the Lamb shall overcome them: for he is Lord of lords, and King of kings: and they that are with him are called, and chosen, and faithful.   Rev 17:14

CONTEXT

And there came one of the seven angels which had the seven vials, and talked with me, saying unto me, Come hither; I will shew unto thee the judgment of the great whore that sitteth upon many waters: With whom the kings of the earth have committed fornication, and the inhabitants of the earth have been made drunk with the wine of her fornication. So he carried me away in the spirit into the wilderness: and I saw a woman sit upon a scarlet coloured beast, full of names of blasphemy, having seven heads and ten horns. And the woman was arrayed in purple and scarlet colour, and decked with gold and precious stones and pearls, having a golden cup in her hand full of abominations and filthiness of her fornication: And upon her forehead was a name written, MYSTERY, BABYLON THE GREAT, THE MOTHER OF HARLOTS AND ABOMINATIONS OF THE EARTH. And I saw the woman drunken with the blood of the saints, and with the blood of the martyrs of Jesus: and when I saw her, I wondered with great admiration. And the angel said unto me, Wherefore didst thou marvel? I will tell thee the mystery of the woman, and of the beast that carrieth her, which hath the seven heads and ten horns. The beast that thou sawest was, and is not; and shall ascend out of the bottomless pit, and go into perdition: and they that dwell on the earth shall wonder, whose names were not written in the book of life from the foundation of the world, when they behold the beast that was, and is not,

165

*and yet is. And here is the mind which hath wisdom. The seven heads are seven mountains, on which the woman sitteth. And there are seven kings: five are fallen, and one is, and the other is not yet come; and when he cometh, he must continue a short space. And the beast that was, and is not, even he is the eighth, and is of the seven, and goeth into perdition. And the ten horns which thou sawest are ten kings, which have received no kingdom as yet; but receive power as kings one hour with the beast. These have one mind, and shall give their power and strength unto the beast. **These shall make war with the Lamb, and the Lamb shall overcome them: for he is Lord of lords, and King of kings: and they that are with him are called, and chosen, and faithful.** And he saith unto me, The waters which thou sawest, where the whore sitteth, are peoples, and multitudes, and nations, and tongues. And the ten horns which thou sawest upon the beast, these shall hate the whore, and shall make her desolate and naked, and shall eat her flesh, and burn her with fire. For God hath put in their hearts to fulfil his will, and to agree, and give their kingdom unto the beast, until the words of God shall be fulfilled. And the woman which thou sawest is that great city, which reigneth over the kings of the earth.*

Rev 17:1-18

International politics can be a great mystery. Even a cursory view of world history reveals an amazing account of perpetual bloodshed and conflict. Jesus said there will be wars and rumors of war until the end of times, but that we should not be troubled (Matt 24:6,7). There is great joy in knowing the Lord will ultimately be victorious, but somehow we must find a way to be settled even in the midst of troubled times.

It is tempting to project the visions of Revelation into current events and view end times as imminent. However, it's a frustrating exercise, even futile. Political scenarios are as unstable as sifting sand. Circumstances today appear to be a direct prophetic fulfillment, only to be cast into doubt by developments occurring tomorrow.

It is a better choice to rest in the ultimate victory of Christ and sense the compassion of Christ for those who are affected by political turmoil. It is better to stand for the peace of Christ and against injustice and the outrage of man's inhumanity one to another.

Dear Lord Jesus:

You are indeed Lord of lords and King of kings, and I do not want to make war with you. What a losing proposition that is. I want to be among those who are with you. I know much of my life was spent resisting you, even ignoring you, yet you have called and chosen me. You are faithful, I am not. The Word says I am called, chosen and faithful. Give me eyes to see your faithfulness in my life Lord. I know that I can only respond to your calling, walk in what you have chosen and live in your faithfulness. It is I in you, not so much you in me, although that is the result.

In you, Lord.

REFLECTION

Being called and chosen is a rich blessing. It is none of me and all of the caller and chooser. It is only for me to respond. I must hear the call, which is not as easy as it sounds. The world has a lot of noise, and I am absorbed in my own pursuits. I can be quiet and hear. I can come to the end of myself and listen. Then I will hear his call. Being chosen also demands a response. He chooses me, then I can choose him. He loves me so that I can love him and others. Being faithful begins to be more than a response; I choose to walk overcoming the world and myself. It was not easy for Jesus and it is not easy for me. Because of him, it is possible.

PRACTICE

Those who are with Christ in overcoming are identified as called, chosen and faithful. As a Christian we have heard and responded to his call. We are now among the chosen and being chosen is not always fun. I remember, and sometimes parrot the words of Tevye as he struggled with the problems of life in *Fiddler on the Roof*. His request of God was: "couldn't you choose someone else for just a little while?"

The issue of being called and chosen is now settled; what remains is faithfulness. Can we be faithful even in the troubles of life? Can we see life as a battle and rest in his victory? It is not easy; it is a battle on the earth and in our own flesh.

Faithfulness is obviously based on faith, and faith is a fruit of the Spirit (Gal 5:22). Without the Holy Spirit we will surely not be faithful. The Holy Spirit gives us the power to overcome, and we can choose to exercise that faith.

The practice of faithfulness may be found in the word—faithfulness. Look up verses speaking of God's faithfulness. Memorize and sing the words of *Great is thy Faithfulness*. Our faith is based on his faithfulness, and we are expected to exercise faith in daily living. It is the reflection of being called and chosen.

---

39. Forsaking Worldliness

And I heard another voice from heaven, saying, Come out of her, my people, that ye be not partakers of her sins, and that ye receive not of her plagues.   Rev 18:4

CONTEXT

And after these things I saw another angel come down from heaven, having great power; and the earth was lightened with his glory. And he cried mightily with a strong voice, saying, Babylon the great is fallen, is fallen, and is become the habitation of devils, and the hold of every foul spirit, and a cage of every unclean and hateful bird. For all nations have drunk of the wine of the wrath of her fornication, and the kings of the earth have committed fornication with her, and the merchants of the earth are waxed rich through the abundance of her delicacies. **And I heard another voice from heaven, saying, Come out of her, my people, that ye be not partakers of her sins, and that ye receive not of her plagues.** For her sins have reached unto heaven, and God hath remembered her iniquities. Reward her even as she rewarded you, and double unto her double according to her works: in the cup which she hath filled fill to her double. How much she hath glorified herself, and lived deliciously, so much torment and sorrow give her: for she saith in her heart, I sit a queen, and am no widow, and shall see no sorrow. Therefore shall her plagues come in one day, death, and mourning, and famine; and she shall be utterly burned with fire: for strong is the Lord God who judgeth her. And the kings of the earth, who have committed fornication and lived deliciously with her, shall bewail her, and lament for her, when they shall see the smoke of her burning, Standing afar *off for the fear of her torment, saying, Alas, alas, that great city*

Babylon, that mighty city! for in one hour is thy judgment
come.   *Rev 18:1-10*

One of the mysteries of eternity is its timelessness. Living in this world of sunrises and sunsets, where there is a sequence to everything, is wonderful but limiting. The defeat of evil is spoken of in the present tense as, *is fallen, is fallen.* Not only is the defeat of evil a present truth in eternity, it is a deep fall. Not much is repeated in scripture. Angels call God holy, holy, holy; and Jesus often begins a discourse with verily, verily. I don't believe the angels nor Jesus stuttered. The redundancy is purposeful; it shows the height of his holiness and the breadth of his truth. Evil is doomed and its sentence is dramatic. The fall is great and can become our strength to come out from the worldliness that carries this condemnation.

Matthew Henry comments; "when the sins of a people reach up to heaven, the wrath of God will reach down to the earth." We cannot constrain our sins nor the sins of the world to the earth. God is omnipresent, and the kingdom of heaven has been declared to be near. It is only because of God's mercy that we stand from day to day.

The Lord is not slack concerning his promise, as some men
count slackness; but is longsuffering to us-ward, not will-
ing that any should perish, but that all should come to re-
pentance.   *2 Pet 3:9*

We can live today knowing evil is fallen; it is the key to forsaking worldliness.

Dear Lord Jesus:

How precious it is for you to call me "my people." I am, and we are, indeed, called by your name. Even in our failures, we are identified in you. Help me to come out, Lord. Keep me from the sins of this world and the consequences they produce. You are the

170

Lord and have put me in a new kingdom of light. I do not need nor desire the darkness. Yet darkness seems to prevail. How can I be a light? How can I be in, but not of the world? How can I minister your grace and not turn others away?

Teach me Lord.

REFLECTION

The word is to come out from among them, but today's struggle is to overcome setbacks and discouragement. The Lord has promised good to me. There seems to be so much to say and so many words of encouragement and yet there is so much discouragement. The word is to come out from among them. I must trust my God and savior in this work. I choose to come out of discouragement and to continue to work in what I know will strengthen me in him. If he chooses to expand my work it will be to his glory. I will read, I will study and I will write. He is the circulation agent.

PRACTICE

I am amazed when Jesus, at the last supper, told Peter he had no part in him unless he washed his feet. Peter's response was, "Wash me all over," but Jesus said: "he that is washed need only to wash his feet" (Matt 13:5-12). What is it with the feet? Why are they so important? Perhaps it is because we walk in the world with our feet. We have a choice of how and where we will walk. Paul didn't experience the washing at the last supper, but he knew the value of walking cleansed.

> *Be ye therefore followers of God, as dear children; And walk in love, as Christ also hath loved us, and hath given himself for us an offering and a sacrifice to God for a sweetsmelling savour.* *Eph 5:1-2*

This I say then, Walk in the Spirit, and ye shall not fulfil the lust of the flesh.   *Gal 5:16*

The fulness of repentance is obedience. It is a willful choice to walk uprightly. It is willful choice to follow after our Savior and walk in love. Even in the flesh, walking takes discipline. A brisk walk in the park has redeeming and restful qualities, but my flesh says wait until tomorrow. It's to cold, to hot, to rainy, to dry—any excuse to avoid taking action. Any excuse to stay in the death that sin has imbedded in our flesh. No, we must wash our feet of worldliness by walking circumspectly, not foolishly but in wisdom (Eph 5:15).

Practice walking by obedience. Choose to go out of your way to help someone. Choose to walk another way when the world attracts you to its temporal and temporary pleasures. Volunteer to visit in a nursing home or serve meals in a shelter. Worldliness will lose its appeal as we learn to walk in love.

---

40. Worthless Treasure

And the fruits that thy soul lusted after are departed from
thee, and all things which were dainty and goodly are departed from thee, and thou shalt find them no more at all.

Rev 18:14

CONTEXT

*And the merchants of the earth shall weep and mourn over
her; for no man buyeth their merchandise any more: The
merchandise of gold, and silver, and precious stones, and
of pearls, and fine linen, and purple, and silk, and scarlet,
and all thyine wood, and all manner vessels of ivory, and
all manner vessels of most precious wood, and of brass,
and iron, and marble, And cinnamon, and odours, and oint-
ments, and frankincense, and wine, and oil, and fine flour,
and wheat, and beasts, and sheep, and horses, and chariots, and slaves, and souls of men.* ***And the fruits that thy
soul lusted after are departed from thee, and all things
which were dainty and goodly are departed from thee,
and thou shalt find them no more at all.*** *The merchants
of these things, which were made rich by her, shall stand
afar off for the fear of her torment, weeping and wailing,
And saying, Alas, alas, that great city, that was clothed in
fine linen, and purple, and scarlet, and decked with gold,
and precious stones, and pearls! For in one hour so great
riches is come to nought. And every shipmaster, and all
the company in ships, and sailors, and as many as trade
by sea, stood afar off, And cried when they saw the smoke
of her burning, saying, What city is like unto this great
city! And they cast dust on their heads, and cried, weeping and wailing, saying, Alas, alas, that great city, wherein
were made rich all that had ships in the sea by reason of
her costliness! for in one hour is she made desolate.*

Rev 18:11-19

173

For thousands of years national differences have been settled mostly with bloody battles. Historical alliances often involved regal marriages, but even that did not prevent violent struggles. I recently read a history of the royal families of Europe and was amazed that hardly any ruler died from natural causes. We are more sophisticated today. Although violence is still an alternative, it seems economic warfare is the principal means for conflict resolution.

Embargos and other economic pressures are the weapons of today. Trade has evolved from a local affair to a national issue. An infamous political electioneering sound-bite was: "it's the economy-stupid." Economics are rapidly becoming an international affair, and trade is a fervent political issue. At the heart of trade is things. Things which are pleasing to the flesh. Things which have only temporal value. We already have so much stuff that storage space rental is a thriving industry. Regardless, the word of the world, convinces us we need even more.

How quickly temporal things can vanish. Few today recall the dramatic speed with which the depression came or the depth of suffering that followed. Truly, the world and all its treasures are a slippery place (Ps 73:18,19).

Desolation of worldly things brings great sorrow; but it is a worldly sorrow formed only in the consequences of sin. No wonder there is no repentance; we live in the symptom, not the disease.

For godly sorrow worketh repentance to salvation not to be repented of: but the sorrow of the world worketh death.
2 Cor 7:10

Dear Lord Jesus:

There are so many seemingly good things I lust after. Help me to recognize lust for what it is, Lord. Help me to look at good things as gifts from you, to be enjoyed but not held or lusted after. Thank you, Lord, for so many comforts, so many good things, so many things to comfort my soul. Mostly, Lord, I thank you for your Word which is food for my soul. Strengthen me in it, Lord. Show me your ways, that I may know you. Show me your glory. The things of earth are temporal. Help me to value the things of eternity and enjoy your gifts in this world.

You are Lord.

REFLECTION

Fruits that satisfy are the words and ways of God. Fruits that satisfy are those of the Holy Spirit. There is no excess of love, joy, peace, gentleness, kindness, meekness, patience and other fruits of the spirit. What do I lust after? It is not just ice cream; I can pass by dainties rather easily. I lust after appreciation, acceptance, honor and other things that build myself up. These things are good but can be destructive in excess. I need to focus on his word in study, in writing and in teaching. Discouragement comes from focusing on acceptance and other self building needs.

PRACTICE

There is a story about a man on his deathbed who negotiated with God to take some earthly possessions with him. He turned all his wealth into gold bars and was buried with them. When he arrived at the gates of heaven, Saint Peter, knowing of the agreement, eyed his heavy burden. With a puzzled look Saint Peter asked, "Why have you brought paving stones?"

God has given us good gifts in this life, including the things of this world. They are gifts to be enjoyed and also to honor the God of our provision. We can't take it with us, yet we still accumulate and hold on to the things of the world as if they are eternal. Scripture clearly tells us that there is a richer treasure.

> *Lay not up for yourselves treasures upon earth, where moth and rust doth corrupt, and where thieves break through and steal: But lay up for yourselves treasures in heaven,*

where neither moth nor rust doth corrupt, and where thieves do not break through nor steal: For where your treasure is, there will your heart be also. Matt 6:19-21

Sadly, my heart does find itself seeking treasures of this earth. My soul frets over the future in the face of uncertainty and insecurity. There is a great tension between the principle that earthly things have little value and the love and desire of our heavenly father to give us good things.

God does not withhold good things from us, but there is a warning label on the package. They must not become our things. As long as we recognize everything we have in this world is a gift, then we can rejoice in the giver. Even Job, who lost every thing, trusted the Lord, as giver and taker. We must hold life and all its goodness very lightly. It is meant to be enjoyed, but not to fulfill our lusts. The enjoyment is to be found in God.

Practice living loosely. Consider your blessings as gifts from God, who loves you. Practice releasing things by giving away something you value. Do it without any recognition. The treasure will be in heaven.

---

41. Vengeance Turned

Rejoice over her, thou heaven, and ye holy apostles and prophets; for God hath avenged you on her.   Rev 18:20

CONTEXT

Rejoice over her, thou heaven, and ye holy apostles and prophets; for God hath avenged you on her. And a mighty angel took up a stone like a great millstone, and cast it into the sea, saying, Thus with violence shall that great city Babylon be thrown down, and shall be found no more at all. And the voice of harpers, and musicians, and of pipers, and trumpeters, shall be heard no more at all in thee; and no craftsman, of whatsoever craft he be, shall be found any more in thee; and the sound of a millstone shall be heard no more at all in thee; And the light of a candle shall shine no more at all in thee; and the voice of the bridegroom and of the bride shall be heard no more at all in thee: for thy merchants were the great men of the earth; for by thy sorceries were all nations deceived. And in her was found the blood of prophets, and of saints, and of all that were slain upon the earth.   Rev 18:20-24

There is nothing joyful about the evil of this world, even in its ultimate judgement. The pain of sinful choices are real; even when justified, there is a sadness about it. Evil works its way in the lives of real people, with real hopes and pains. There is a point of rejoicing in myself knowing I escaped the horrible judgement of sin, but only by the grace of God.

God says rejoice in his vengeance. My heart wants to weep over those who choose his vengeance; and it is a choice. How sad it is they could not choose the grace of salvation.

God says rejoice, and I can rejoice over the defeat of evil. Whatever judgement is reserved for evil and its perpetrators, it is not only justified, but appropriate. The world would mourn, but the people of God and all of heaven rejoice.

A cause for rejoicing can be found in the irrecoverable fall of evil. There is joy in knowing that the righteous will no longer be afflicted by the enemies of God. There is rejoicing in its permanence. Deception is exposed, and persecution of the godly is revealed for what it is—evil.

Judgement may be justified and appropriate, but there may be a tear behind the joy of its expression. God will wipe away even those tears; and we can respond with the fulness of joy, to see the end of evil and its terrible work in the earth.

Dear Lord Jesus:

The Lord God is just in all that he does. In you he has made mercy and grace live so that the vengeance of God can be turned. Praise to you, Lord, for bearing this vengeance in yourself and making it possible for me to know grace and acceptance. Thank you, Lord, for saving me. I know the horror of sin and of vengeance. I learned the fear of God in it. I know the great love with which you love me and am learning to love with your love. Today is a day of rejoicing in your love and because of your salvation. It is fresh every morning.

Saved in love.

REFLECTION

How can anyone rejoice over vengeance? The Lord proclaims vengeance is his. I am told to pray for and bless those who persecute me, for his sake. It is hard to understand the wrath of God when you have been nurtured in his mercy and goodness. I know that I deserve wrath but receive mercy. What is the difference between me and those who receive his wrath? In the flesh there is no difference. Even in the church there is the fruit of the flesh. Israel was rebellious; and today spiritual leaders fall and churches split or seem like a business. Grace is truly amazing. Mercy is without justification, I only believe.

PRACTICE

Yesterday a violent criminal was sentenced to death. How am I to respond? One reaction is, well he got what was coming to him—an eye for an eye and a tooth for a tooth. Or, thank God I am not like those other sinners. Those reactions comes right out of my flesh and reveal the depth of my own sin. How am I to respond? I can mourn with those who suffered the violence of his crime. I can understand their cry for vengeance which comes directly from their pain.

Today the victim's family responded with, "We forgive him." What a difference there is between a reaction and a response. Now I have to face my own reaction. I am indeed like those other sinners—there but for the grace of God am I. God be merciful to me, a sinner. The pharisee in me must give way to the publican in me. My reaction must give way to a response.

Vengeance is turned in forgiveness. Even the pain of injustice is tempered in forgiveness so healing can begin. Without forgiveness, even vengeance will not satisfy the reaction in myself. Unforgiveness will root itself in choking bitterness, and the violence of evil will be extended, even enlarged.

God's vengeance is a reality, but it's tempered with grace and mercy. Our vengeance will overshadow God's and is without grace, often returning to its source. Let God's vengeance live, its anticipation should cause us to learn the fear of God.

> *If thou, LORD, shouldest mark iniquities, O Lord, who shall stand? But there is forgiveness with thee, that thou mayest be feared.*   *Ps 130:3-4*

We can turn to his forgiveness and live in that joy. I can rejoice over vengeance if it causes me to turn to his forgiveness; and the expression of my rejoicing should be forgiveness.

Vengeance can be turned by forgiveness. There are plenty of opportunities to forgive. Respond, don't react; let forgiveness flow in your own life. Mourn the pain of being hurt, but seek forgiveness. Forgiveness is a grace and a choice; it is a response that acknowledges your own forgiveness in Christ.

Even if you have not been hurt today, consider injuries of the past or even offences you have taken up for others—forgive. Begin by just saying in your heart, "I choose to forgive." Let God work the miracle that he has worked in your own life—forgiveness.

42. Becoming Praise

And a voice came out of the throne, saying, Praise our God, all ye his servants, and ye that fear him, both small and great.   Rev 19:5

CONTEXT

*And after these things I heard a great voice of much people in heaven, saying, Alleluia; Salvation, and glory, and honour, and power, unto the Lord our God: For true and righteous are his judgments: for he hath judged the great whore, which did corrupt the earth with her fornication, and hath avenged the blood of his servants at her hand. And again they said, Alleluia. And her smoke rose up for ever and ever. And the four and twenty elders and the four beasts fell down and worshipped God that sat on the throne, saying, Amen; Alleluia. **And a voice came out of the throne, saying, Praise our God, all ye his servants, and ye that fear him, both small and great.** Rev 19:1-5*

There is a crowd in heaven and they have a great voice. It is a voice of praise. If I could even begin to picture this crowd of re-deemed sinners, gladness would fill my heart. There is a crowd; but it is not crowded. There is always room for one more. Oh, to be in that number, when the saints praise with a great voice. The praise is for salvation. It is salvation that magnifies his glory, and honor, and power. It is a praise we can express today; but it will be so much richer in the fulness of its promise.

He is true and he is righteous, even in the judgement of evil. My praise is in his salvation and for deliverance from the horror of judgement whose smoke goes up forever. Will we always be able to see the smoke of his judgement, even in eternity, even in the new creation? If so, it will always be a source of praise to the Lord our God. Today, just reading about it builds a sense of praise, knowing that my salvation is eternal, just as the judgement of evil is eternal. When Jesus walked this earth, a voice came out of heaven.

And there came a voice out of the cloud, saying, This is my beloved Son: hear him. Luke 9:35

Hear him, hear the Word of the Lord, praise him. Recognize the miracle of salvation and the power and mercy of God. Be one who knows the fear of God and one who can rejoice in his great salvation.

Dear Lord Jesus:

Lord, you are the praise of God. You are great and greatly to be praised. You have come out of the throne of God and humbled yourself to become like us. You overcame death and hell so that I might live in the praise of your glory. God is worthy of praise and you are what makes his praise worthy. Your Holy Spirit speaks in me, and my spirit is alive because of the Spirit of God. My spirit says praise; my flesh resists, but I choose to overcome my flesh. I choose to praise. I choose to agree with my spirit in you. Praise to God and to you, his lamb.

In the spirit of praise.

REFLECTION

Praise is perfected in service; and it is rooted in the fear of God. Fear becomes love, and the expression of love becomes service to God and to his body on earth. Praise is presenting myself to him, raising my arms in submission, audibly speaking his worthiness, singing with his joy and recognizing his presence. The voice coming out of the throne is a voice of authority. Praise is a matter of obedience; it is a command from the throne of God. It is not a burdensome command, it is a joyful command; one that brings joy to the throne and to his servants who fear him. It is a bilateral blessing, one flowing both ways.

PRACTICE

Our God is praiseworthy and our salvation compels us to exercise praise. Song is a powerful expression that enlarges the habitation of our God and builds us up in the spirit. In the old testament, singers were appointed to teach others to praise (II Chron. 23:13). Singing praises is not just a haphazard activity. One of the attributes of God is his orderliness. Scripture has an order for singing and for expressions that are designed to accomplish specific purposes in our lives and in ministry to others.

> *Speaking to yourselves in psalms and hymns and spiritual songs, singing and making melody in your heart to the Lord; Giving thanks always for all things unto God and the Father in the name of our Lord Jesus Christ; Submitting yourselves one to another in the fear of God.* Eph 5:18-21

The work of singing praises brings edification, enlightenment and encouragement for the body. Three types of singing are recommended; psalms, hymns and spiritual songs. Besides expressing praise to our God, each type has a specific purpose in our own lives.

Psalms: Singing psalms is like hiding his word in our heart. When we sing the scripture we are singing his word to him. His words edify our life.

Hymns: Singing hymns is like instructing our heart; it is establishing our heritage in God. The words of hymns enlighten our life.

Spiritual Songs: Singing spiritual songs is like building up our heart. The words of spiritual songs encourage our life.

183

There are some things which are earthly and some heavenly. Singing happens to be both. The gift of singing may be unique to humanity, but it is eternal.

> *I will sing of the mercies of the LORD for ever: with my mouth will I make known thy faithfulness to all generations.* Ps 89:1

Practice praise by obeying the Word of God—sing psalms, hymns and spiritual songs. Then your heart will hide his word, your mind will be instructed and your soul built up. Then praise will do its work of enlarging God in the earth and in our hearts. It is an eternal activity.

---

43. In Preparation

Let us be glad and rejoice, and give honour to him: for the marriage of the Lamb is come, and his wife hath made herself ready.   Rev 19:7

CONTEXT

And I heard as it were the voice of a great multitude, and as the voice of many waters, and as the voice of mighty thunderings, saying, Alleluia: for the Lord God omnipotent reigneth. **Let us be glad and rejoice, and give honour to him: for the marriage of the Lamb is come, and his wife hath made herself ready.** *And to her was granted that she should be arrayed in fine linen, clean and white: for the fine linen is the righteousness of saints. And he saith unto me, Write, Blessed are they which are called unto the marriage supper of the Lamb. And he saith unto me, These are the true sayings of God. And I fell at his feet to worship him. And he said unto me, See thou do it not: I am thy fellowservant, and of thy brethren that have the testimony of Jesus: worship God: for the testimony of Jesus is the spirit of prophecy.*   Rev 19:6-10

The voice of a multitude is normally just noise; but when it is unity then it becomes a single voice. All of heaven is in unity on one point—the Lord God omnipotent reigns. Christ reigns today and has reigned forever, but sin and its disunity lives as well. How marvelous will be the sound of unity when evil is finally put away.

The voice of unity will become prophetic fulfillment in the marriage of the Lamb. Marriage itself was created by God to be unity.

For we are members of his body, of his flesh, and of his bones. For this cause shall a man leave his father and

185

*mother, and shall be joined unto his wife, and they two
shall be one flesh. This is a great mystery: but I speak
concerning Christ and the church.*   *Eph 5:30-32*

We live in the mystery of marriage today, and it can be a place
of gladness and rejoicing. Unfortunately, the voice of division often robs the gladness. What a shame. Not only do we miss great
joy, but the image of our Lord and Savior is tarnished. We are
tarnished individually and as a body, but Christ is our righteousness. Individually we must come to him for salvation and for the
cleansing that covers the stain of sin. No wonder the messenger
says, "Write." There can be no greater message of blessing than
the hope of reconciliation and restoration—the fullness of unity.

Dear Lord Jesus:

Thank you, Lord, for the hope of unity and restoration. To you
belongs honor and we can rejoice and be glad. There is so much
disunity, Lord, so much brokenness in the body and in the bride.
How do we make our self ready? I know many things that can be
done: prayer, praise and holy living are among them. Preparation,
however, is a continuing process. I am glad and I do rejoice when
I focus on you in my life. When I look around at the disunity, I
mourn. Turn our mourning into joy, Lord. Wipe away our tears,
heal us, give us white garments of your holiness.
Seeking you.

REFLECTION

Let us be glad and rejoice implies I have a choice. I can see the
hand of God in our broken world and in my broken life. I need to
look and then choose to rejoice. I can see hope as I understand
God's plan for restoration of unity; and I am glad. It is faith, hope
and love doing their great work again. Faith that he is in the very
midst of our brokenness, hope in his restoration and knowing his

love in what will be my today. Praise to God who is alive, who has a purpose and a plan. He loves me with his perfect love, so I will rejoice and be glad.

PRACTICE

It looks like there is going to be a wedding. When I got married the preparations took many months. I know couples whose planning and preparation took several years.

There is something very special about a wedding. Who can imagine the time, expense and emotional energy individuals and families invest in the day? We sponsored a booth at a bridal fair recently and noticed that there were many elaborate booths, each proclaiming a necessity for the wedding day. Tuxedos, gowns, restaurants, honeymoon locales, florists, limo rentals and wedding planners were the theme of the day. In our booth, we offered couples an opportunity to attend *Intimate Life* seminars prior to and after the wedding. Our booth was the only one focused on the marriage. No one else seemed to want to talk about the marriage, only the wedding. The intensity of the effort that goes into a wedding seems to overshadow the marriage, yet it is the marriage that must last. Earthly marriages are purposed for a lifetime. The heavenly marriage is for eternity.

The marriage of the Lamb will be a celebration that outshines any wedding we could plan on this earth. Even royal weddings, as grand as they are, will fade into nothing compared to the heavenly marriage.

God has sent out the invitations and an RSVP is required. A positive response to his calling will begin the time of preparation with garments of his righteousness.

Now we are in the time of preparation. Now, all that comes into our lives can be seen as preparation for that great day. Even troubles and tribulations are here for our preparation. Jesus assured us that we would have troubles and should be of good cheer (John 16:33). Paul says tribulations should be our glory (Rom

5:3). Hard sayings, but if you have ever been through earthly wedding planning, the difficulties may not be so unrealistic.

For those of us who are married, the unity of that relationship is the place to practice preparation for the eternal marriage. For the unmarried, preparation is also found in godly relationships. We can find unity of spirit and heart in the body of Christ. We can face tribulation as a couple in marriage, and we can face it in the unity of the body of Christ.

Practice preparation by honoring relationships. It is not easy. Our flesh and the enemy of our soul want isolation. We must choose to be open and vulnerable, but that only comes with trust. First, we must choose to be with others, to hear their heart and mind. Be with people, go to church not to just meet an obligation, but to meet a real living person. Visit a friend, just be available. Relationships will help us grow so that we can live fully in that vibrant relationship for which we are eternally called—the body of Christ.

---

44. In His Name

... and he that sat upon him was called Faithful and True,
... and his name is called The Word of God. ... a name
written, KING OF KINGS, AND LORD OF LORDS.

Rev 19:11p,13b,16b

CONTEXT

And I saw heaven opened, and behold a white horse; **and
he that sat upon him was called Faithful and True,** *and
in righteousness he doth judge and make war. His eyes
were as a flame of fire, and on his head were many crowns;
and he had a name written, that no man knew, but he himself. And he was clothed with a vesture dipped in blood:*
and his name is called The Word of God. *And the armies
which were in heaven followed him upon white horses,
clothed in fine linen, white and clean. And out of his mouth
goeth a sharp sword, that with it he should smite the nations: and he shall rule them with a rod of iron: and he
treadeth the winepress of the fierceness and wrath of Almighty God. And he hath on his vesture and on his thigh* **a
name written, KING OF KINGS, AND LORD OF
LORDS.**

Rev 19:11-16

The groom who was a Lamb has become our champion. Now
he judges in righteousness and, not only defends his own, he ag-
gressively pursues those who have chosen to stand against him.
He is called faithful and true; and these names are now expressions
of his character. Every word of God will become reality.

He has many names, but there is still much we cannot begin to
know about him. Some day we will see him as he is, in the fulness
of his glory, but we will still find that he is unsearchable. There is
a quality of our Lord and Savior that will always be beyond the

understanding of his creation. It is a name, a quality, only he will know.

Part of his glory is dipped in blood. There has been much righteous blood shed over the centuries; but it is his blood which defines his own. Those who follow him are clothed in the purity of his righteousness, his blood. All the blood of the prophets and the saints could not bring this to pass, but the blood of the Lamb, the Son of God has made it possible. We can follow him today in the fellowship of his suffering, and we can follow him tomorrow in his victory over evil.

The fear of God which became love when we chose his salvation, will become terror for those who reject his grace. We cannot minimize the fierceness of his wrath; it should cause us to praise him and to learn to experience the significance of his name.

Dear Lord Jesus:

"Faithful and True," it is a wonderful name; even the "Word of God" is wonderful. What about "King of Kings and Lord of Lords?" Now you are starting to meddle, Lord. I still want my way, Lord. How can I call you truth or faithfulness without seeking your lordship? You humbled yourself because you love me, and you saved me from the death my way brings. Yet I still want my way. I am a sucker for significance, for recognition and affirmation. All of these are seemingly good and encouraged; but only within your lordship, your gifting, are they valid and lasting.

Direct me, Lord.

REFLECTION

The names of God proclaim his wonder. He is wonderful, lord, true, faithful, king and a long list of other glorious callings which proclaim his wonder. I can see his wonder in the Word because he is the Word. I especially love it when I seem to have spiritual insight or direction from his Word. He is wonderful and there are wondrous things in his Word. What makes them wonderful is that they are as true and faithful as is he. The words are alive. The Holy Spirit speaks of Jesus, the Word, and his words become life in me. It is a miracle, it is wondrous.

PRACTICE

It is hard to think of a name as having much meaning these days. We select our children's names because they are cute or fashionable. We name companies with letters or meaningless abstractions. Names have just become tags; we might as well use numbers—perhaps we will some day. Even nicknames which say something special about the person, are losing their appeal as we strive for sameness and conformity.

No wonder when we pray in Jesus' name there is no authority. Heal my headache, in Jesus' name. Let me win the lottery, in Jesus' name. "InJesusNameAmen" has become one word, a word that only says we are through praying.

Scripture calls us to prayer, even encourages us to pray without ceasing (I Thess 5:17). We are also warned about self-righteous prayer and prayer that is hindered by presumptuous living. Surely we can pray anything so long as we invoke the power behind the magical name of Jesus. No wonder we are often discouraged to enter a vibrant prayer life.

Is it vain to trivialize the name of our Lord? The third commandment says don't do it, and also has a consequence associated with it.

> *Thou shalt not take the name of the LORD thy God in vain;*
> *for the LORD will not hold him guiltless that taketh his*
> *name in vain.* *Exod 20:7*

There is a lot of guilt being carried in the Church today. Some of it is certainly justified, but much is irrational and crippling. Perhaps the extent of unresolved guilt is just a symptom of a true illness, that of trivializing what God has given meaning to—his name.

191

What is the response to sin? First, confession, agree with God that his name is powerful and true. Second, repentance, just stop doing it. Unfortunately, "InJesusNameAmen" has become a habit, but habits can be broken. The usual way to break a habit is to substitute an alternative behavior.

Practice repentance; stop praying in Jesus name for a while. Just say amen, or pray in Christ's name. Make a list of the names of God and take turns praying in each of those names. But first, pray for the Holy Spirit to teach you how to pray. You can even pray that prayer "In Jesus Name." He did not deny his disciples when they made the same request.

45. Victory in Jesus

And the beast was taken, and with him the false prophet
that wrought miracles before him, ...   Rev 19:20a

CONTEXT

*And I saw an angel standing in the sun; and he cried with
a loud voice, saying to all the fowls that fly in the midst of
heaven, Come and gather yourselves together unto the
supper of the great God; That ye may eat the flesh of kings,
and the flesh of captains, and the flesh of mighty men, and
the flesh of horses, and of them that sit on them, and the
flesh of all men, both free and bond, both small and great.
And I saw the beast, and the kings of the earth, and their
armies, gathered together to make war against him that
sat on the horse, and against his army. **And the beast was
taken, and with him the false prophet that wrought
miracles before him,** with which he deceived them that
had received the mark of the beast, and them that worshipped his image. These both were cast alive into a lake
of fire burning with brimstone. And the remnant were slain
with the sword of him that sat upon the horse, which sword
proceeded out of his mouth: and all the fowls were filled
with their flesh.*   *Rev 19:17-21*

It's not a good thing to lose a war. I have seen the destruction,
displacement of families, death and poverty that result from war.
Modern warfare tends to isolate us from its horrors, but the reality
is—war is hell, especially for the loser.

One of my life experiences includes being a witness to the
military tribunals following World War II. These were judgements
of men who had been actively involved with the atrocities of war.
They had been leaders, or as the Bible would say, mighty men.
The defense of, "they were only following orders," fell on deaf

ears. Each person was judged individually, and several were sentenced to death. Very few were acquitted, and even the few acquittals left a bitter taste in the mouths of those who had seen comrades fall.

The spiritual war has no less of a consequence. Death, destruction, broken families, conflict, and poverty of soul are all as real as if it were a physical war. For sure, it is not a good thing to lose this war. The judgements are eternal. After a physical war, there is often an effort to restore the losing nation. Not so in the spiritual war; judgement is complete and permanent.

It's not a good thing to lose a war, especially the spiritual war. But for the overcomer, there is eternal victory in the King of Kings and Lord of Lords.

Dear Lord Jesus:

The Word, your Word, is the sword that overcomes and also destroys those who hurt, kill and deceive. Praise you, Lord, for you will set all things right. There is hope in this life and in eternity. You were victorious on the earth and will be victorious in the heavenlies. You have given me life in the Word, and that Word is a sword. It is an instrument to build hope and bring life to those who will believe. The soul and the spirit is separated from one another, Lord, so that the spirit may prevail. The spirit is life; my flesh is death. Thank you, Lord, for the difference.

Entering life.

REFLECTION

What a glorious hope we have; no more sorrow, no more death, no more deception, no more tears or even the remembrance of the ugly former things. Praise to my God who is not only victorious but able to restore. Praise to my God who does more than destroy evil and deception; he fills life with love. It is hard to perceive that hope, living in the brokenness of this world, but it is true. There are glimpses of his glory in this present time, if I just look. The beauty of today, the quietness of the morning, speaks of my glorious God and his wonderful Savior.

PRACTICE

> *He will swallow up death in victory; and the Lord GOD will wipe away tears from off all faces; and the rebuke of his people shall he take away from off all the earth: for the LORD hath spoken it. And it shall be said in that day, Lo, this is our God; we have waited for him, and he will save us: this is the LORD; we have waited for him, we will be glad and rejoice in his salvation.* Isa 25:8-9

One of the tears which God will wipe away, will be for those who have rejected the grace of his salvation. It is a cause for mourning today and also a call to go and tell of his great love. If earthly war should suggest anything it, is the horror of sin. It should also remind us of the dreadful fate of those who continue in its deception.

Our salvation is great and worthy to be celebrated. We are, and will be *glad and rejoice in his salvation.* Victory in Jesus, the perfection of salvation. Victory in Jesus, the strength to live in hope today. Victory in Jesus, the peace that passes understanding. The victory may not be complete in the world today, but Christ declared *it is finished* from the cross. Christ's victory has brought us who believe, peace with God. In Christ we can find the peace of God in daily life.

I can live in victory. The reality of eternity can become a living truth in my life today. The tears of battle, even defeat and failure may exist. Nevertheless, I can find a quiet rest in my soul that causes victory to rise up. Even with tearful eyes, I can declare victory in Christ Jesus; and it is not a hollow pronouncement. The Holy Spirit makes it a reality.

In whom ye also trusted, after that ye heard the word of truth, the gospel of your salvation: in whom also after that ye believed, ye were sealed with that holy Spirit of promise, Which is the earnest of our inheritance until the redemption of the purchased possession, unto the praise of his glory.   *Eph 1:13-14*

When challenges interrupt your life, and they are always uninvited intrusions, let his peace fill your response. One of the best ways to defeat a deceiver is to ignore him. Resist the enemy of your soul and he will flee (James 4:7). This is not a casual instruction. A defeated foe will always run when he is exposed.

Practice the experience of his victory—relax. It is okay to rest, God did. Realize resting is more than just sitting down, it is releasing the frustrations and troubles of life to God. When we rest in Christ we may even find the power to rejoice in the things with which life interrupts our living.

196

46. Cleansing Judgement

And the sea gave up the dead which were in it; and death
and hell delivered up the dead which were in them: and
they were judged every man according to their works.

Rev 20:13

CONTEXT

*And I saw an angel come down from heaven, having the
key of the bottomless pit and a great chain in his hand.
And he laid hold on the dragon, that old serpent, which is
the Devil, and Satan, and bound him a thousand years,
And cast him into the bottomless pit, and shut him up, and
set a seal upon him, that he should deceive the nations no
more, till the thousand years should be fulfilled: and after
that he must be loosed a little season. And I saw thrones,
and they sat upon them, and judgment was given unto them:
and I saw the souls of them that were beheaded for the
witness of Jesus, and for the word of God, and which had
not worshipped the beast, neither his image, neither had
received his mark upon their foreheads, or in their hands;
and they lived and reigned with Christ a thousand years.
But the rest of the dead lived not again until the thousand
years were finished. This is the first resurrection. Blessed
and holy is he that hath part in the first resurrection: on
such the second death hath no power, but they shall be
priests of God and of Christ, and shall reign with him a
thousand years. And when the thousand years are expired,
Satan shall be loosed out of his prison, And shall go out to
deceive the nations which are in the four quarters of the
earth, Gog and Magog, to gather them together to battle:
the number of whom is as the sand of the sea. And they
went up on the breadth of the earth, and compassed the
camp of the saints about, and the beloved city: and fire*

came down from God out of heaven, and devoured them. And the devil that deceived them was cast into the lake of fire and brimstone, where the beast and the false prophet are, and shall be tormented day and night for ever and ever. And I saw a great white throne, and him that sat on it, from whose face the earth and the heaven fled away; and there was found no place for them. And I saw the dead, small and great, stand before God; and the books were opened: and another book was opened, which is the book of life: and the dead were judged out of those things which were written in the books, according to their works. **And the sea gave up the dead which were in it; and death and hell delivered up the dead which were in them: and they were judged every man according to their works.** *And death and hell were cast into the lake of fire. This is the second death. And whosoever was not found written in the book of life was cast into the lake of fire.*

Rev 20:1-15

In the garden, the work of Satan was to deceive man. That work lives in me as iniquity. My deception was dealt with at the cross of my Lord and Savior, Jesus Christ. Now Satan's work is to deceive the nations. The evidence of that work is the horror of war and persecution of the godly which continues until the day of judgement.

Judgement. It sounds ominous, and it is. It is ominous because the sentence is death. We know about the first death; and as much as we fear it, we realize there is hope. Not so with the second death; it is death without hope. There is no light, only the darkness of a hopeless eternity.

When Paul preached the doctrine *of judgement to come*, Felix, the Governor of Judah, trembled (Acts 24:25). We, even as believers, should tremble; but we should also rejoice in the salvation of our Christ. He has delivered us from the judgement of death. His judgement is for our cleansing. His judgement is to consume our dead works so we may stand before God in his righteousness.

Like the first death, the first judgement has hope. We are judged against the gospel, and by faith we find blessing. The second judgement is against the law, and by works the lost find cursing—the second death. The joy of salvation is that we escape the second judgement, living by grace and not by works.

Dear Lord Jesus:

It is said that only death and taxes are sure; but it is not true, both shall cease. Life is the only sure thing for those who are written in your book of life. Physical death is only a passage to eternal life. Praise to you, Lord, for creation and for preserving your created purpose of life on this earth. Thank you, Lord, for the assurance of your love and the Holy Spirit which matures me in your love. Thank you, Lord, for the book of life and for making it possible for me to enter life eternal.

Yours forever.

REFLECTION

The dead are raised for one purpose, judgement. I look forward to the judgement seat of Christ; in it all of my dead works will be consumed. God's judgement is fearsome because each individual's eternity is determined in it. Praise to my Lord who has made me clean and righteous in himself. I do not face judgement that condemns, rather, I face judgement that cleanses. This is the good work that you will perform and complete in your day. I know whom I believe and have the Holy Spirit in me to help me grow toward that great day. Today he is settling me in the hope of his soon return.

PRACTICE

When the Bible speaks of cleansing, it is generally associated with healing the terrible disease of leprosy. When Jesus healed the blind or deaf, it was a blessing, but when he healed leprosy, it was called a cleansing (Luke 5:14). We are all lepers, carrying about the dreadful disease called sin. Praise to our Savior, there is a cleansing for this disease as well.

If we confess our sins, he is faithful and just to forgive us our sins, and to cleanse us from all unrighteousness. If we say that we have not sinned, we make him a liar, and his word is not in us.   *1 Jn 1:9-10*

Practice the cleansing judgement of Christ by confession. We know we are sinners, but it takes courage to admit it. Pray like the publican, *God be merciful to me, a sinner* (Luke 18:13). Christ is faithful to his Word; and his cleansing will enable our good works to show forth as his righteousness in the day of judgement.

47. Declare Renewal

And he that sat upon the throne said, Behold, I make all
things new. And he said unto me, Write: for these words
are true and faithful.   Rev 21:5

CONTEXT

*And I saw a new heaven and a new earth: for the first
heaven and the first earth were passed away; and there
was no more sea. And I John saw the holy city, new Jerusalem, coming down from God out of heaven, prepared as a
bride adorned for her husband. And I heard a great voice
out of heaven saying, Behold, the tabernacle of God is with
men, and he will dwell with them, and they shall be his
people, and God himself shall be with them, and be their
God. And God shall wipe away all tears from their eyes;
and there shall be no more death, neither sorrow, nor crying, neither shall there be any more pain: for the former
things are passed away.* **And he that sat upon the throne
said, Behold, I make all things new. And he said unto
me, Write: for these words are true and faithful.**
Rev 21:1-5

The whole of scripture describes a glorious process of restoration. It begins in the book of Genesis at the fall and concludes in
the book of Revelation with a "new heaven and a new earth." The
turning point in God's plan for restoration is redemption through
the sacrifice of our Lord, Jesus Christ.

Restoration is a major theme of scripture; unfortunately, it seems
to be a cyclical process. The historical books of the Old Testament
describe the Nation of Israel in repeated cycles of repentance and
restoration, only to fall again to the place of calling out to God.

Ups and downs are also typical in the New Testament, in church
history, and are apparent in the life we live today. Most secular

approaches to overcoming dependencies or life difficulties is limited to the process of recovery. Just being recovered is as good as it gets. God wants us to go beyond recovery to restoration. But even restoration is limited to the fallen resources of today. God has a better plan—it is called renewal—he will make everything new. The beauty of God's plan is even recovery and restoration are passed away with all their pain. An even greater beauty is, *God himself shall be with them, and be their God.*

God sought the fellowship of Adam in the garden, and even today we can have a sense of his presence through the Holy Spirit. In renewal, he will dwell with us, and we shall be his people. We are no more *a people*, but have become *his people* (1 Peter 2:10). These words can be written in our lives today as we live knowing he is true and faithful to his Word.

Dear Lord Jesus:

I asked for a word from you, Lord, and waited, is the word to write? I can write, Lord, and I know that what comes from you will be true and faithful. Help me, Lord, to learn to write and to communicate your words so that others are blessed. You are on the throne of my life. Sometimes I don't act like it; but it is more that I don't know your direction, or am discouraged with my own measure of success. Praise you, Lord, you know the end from the beginning. Help me to live and write your words.

Hearing and listening

REFLECTION

His words are true and faithful, but my ability to communicate them loses something in the translation. Discouragement is a product of the curse, but I do not live under the curse. I live under grace, by faith toward hope. God is currently making things new, and he wants his true and faithful word to be shared. Does he want to use me? I think so. How does he want to use me? Is it writing or just being available to my neighbor. In the meantime I will do both. I will write, I will work at loving those whom he brings into my life. He is true and faithful and will direct my path.

PRACTICE

In order to appreciate the glories of redemption and the process of restoration, we must first have a sense of the magnitude of loss which resulted from the fall. The consequences and horrors of sin are evident every day; and we can find our desperate need for God in its midst.

God had a plan for creation and for its redemption, restoration and renewal even before the fall. Redemption is the turning point in the whole of God's creation plan. We are fallen, and God himself has provided for our redemption in the Lord Jesus Christ, his only son. In Christ we enable the process of restoration and see the hope of renewal.

It is Christ who has broken the power of sin and rescued us from destruction. It is the Holy Spirit who is at work enabling our personal restoration and our defense while the work is in progress. The Holy Spirit also enlightens us regarding our inheritance in the kingdom of God and the new creation we have in Christ.

> *Therefore if any man be in Christ, he is a new creature: old things are passed away; behold, all things are become new. And all things are of God, who hath reconciled us to himself by Jesus Christ, and hath given to us the ministry of reconciliation;* 2 Cor 5:17-18

Renewal is a great hope, but like all things eternal it has a present tense as well as some futuristic expectation. Eternity has a quality of being true yesterday, today and forever (Heb 13:8).

The expression of renewal in this life is called reconciliation. The gospel is the word of reconciliation, and being reconciled we are to share this good news as we live its truth.

Reconciliation means to come together. It is a restoration of unity that has been broken by offense.

Practice reconciliation; if there are any whom you have offended, go to them and offer reconciliation in humility. If you have been offended, forgive, then seek reconciliation. It may not be received, it may not even be noticed. That's okay, our calling is the ministry of reconciliation. An offense is not even a necessary a part of the process.

48. A Godly Heritage

... and names written thereon, which are the names of the twelve tribes of the children of Israel: ... and in them the names of the twelve apostles of the Lamb.

Rev 21:12b,14b

CONTEXT

*And he said unto me, It is done. I am Alpha and Omega, the beginning and the end. I will give unto him that is athirst of the fountain of the water of life freely. He that overcometh shall inherit all things; and I will be his God, and he shall be my son. But the fearful, and unbelieving, and the abominable, and murderers, and whoremongers, and sorcerers, and idolaters, and all liars, shall have their part in the lake which burneth with fire and brimstone: which is the second death. And there came unto me one of the seven angels which had the seven vials full of the seven last plagues, and talked with me, saying, Come hither, I will shew thee the bride, the Lamb's wife. And he carried me away in the spirit to a great and high mountain, and shewed me that great city, the holy Jerusalem, descending out of heaven from God, Having the glory of God: and her light was like unto a stone most precious, even like a jasper stone, clear as crystal; And had a wall great and high, and had twelve gates, and at the gates twelve angels, **and names written thereon, which are the names of the twelve tribes of the children of Israel:** On the east three gates; on the north three gates; on the south three gates; and on the west three gates. And the wall of the city had twelve foundations, **and in them the names of the twelve apostles of the Lamb.** And he that talked with me had a golden reed to measure the city, and the gates thereof, and the wall thereof. And the city lieth foursquare, and the length is as*

large as the breadth: and he measured the city with the reed, twelve thousand furlongs. The length and the breadth and the height of it are equal. And he measured the wall thereof, an hundred and forty and four cubits, according to the measure of a man, that is, of the angel.
Rev 21:6-17

It is done. The eternal past and eternal future all come together in a present tense. God called himself "I Am" and our Lord, the beginning and end, proclaims it is done. The present tense of God's name and Christ's work enable a future tense expression of our inheritance and adoption as sons. His living water fills this life and lets us taste and live today as if there is a tomorrow, his tomorrow—eternity.

Horror of horrors, the second death. There but for the grace of God go I. What a tragedy for those who reject his great mercy and grace. It is commonly said mercy is not getting what you deserve, and grace is getting what you don't deserve. Thank God for living waters.

The holy Jerusalem may be a mystery, but its gates and foundations are not. It is our heritage. It is a heritage of family, based on Christ himself—the foundational cornerstone.

Now therefore ye are no more strangers and foreigners, but fellowcitizens with the saints, and of the household of God; And are built upon the foundation of the apostles and prophets, Jesus Christ himself being the chief corner stone;
Eph 2:19-20

Dear Lord Jesus:

You are the Lord. What a heritage you have made for me. A heritage of your chosen people and a heritage of your elect. Praise to you, Lord, for twelve tribes and twelve apostles. Praise you for your true and faithful word which has come through these people. You still speak through people, Lord, but it is based on the truth of

206

your Word. Thank you, Lord, for the scripture, which speaks of our heritage in the tribes and our faith by the apostles. It is all your work and your revelation. Because of your love and Word, we are not consumed in deception.

True to the truth.

REFLECTION

Twelve tribes and twelve apostles; all men with abilities and failures. The Lord has chosen earthen vessels to show forth his glory. My spiritual heritage is based on a bunch of brothers who sold one of their own into slavery. It is based on a group of men who bickered and even denied the one whom God sent, his only Son. It gives me hope in God to see they were like me. This earthen vessel sure has its problems and has tarnished the name of my savior through poor choices. Yet, he loves me and lets me live and minister in his name and in his Word.

PRACTICE

The mercy of God is richly expressed through our heritage in the Old Testament. The grace of God finds mercy fulfilled by grace in the New Testament. It is a godly heritage. The two words, mercy and grace most often appear together with peace in Scripture.

> *Grace be with you, mercy, and peace, from God the Father, and from the Lord Jesus Christ, the Son of the Father, in truth and love.* II Jn 1:3

We have a heritage of peace expressed through grace and mercy. We can read about the failures of the sons of Jacob and those who precede and follow them. It is a sad story of victory and defeat until we recognize it is our own story. Now it is personal, and we can praise God for his mercy in our own life. He didn't give up on them, and he will not give up on us.

We can read the expression of grace through the words of the apostles. Because of mercy and grace we are family; and those who first experienced his grace call us to *know the love of Christ, which passeth knowledge, that ye might be filled with all the fulness of God* (Eph 3:19). What peace can come from understanding the depth of his mercy, that picks us up, and the height of his grace, that raises us up.

Experience living in our great heritage. Let the peace of God rule in your life. Peace is something we can "let" happen. It can come from being thankful (Col 3:15).

Practice letting peace rule by expressing thanks. Thank God in prayer for mercy and grace. Thank others in your family for their part in your life. Write a letter to someone who has added to your life; thank God for them. It is family. It is love—the love of God.

---

49. Seeing His Glory

And the city had no need of the sun, neither of the moon, to shine in it: for the glory of God did lighten it, and the Lamb is the light thereof.   Rev 21:23

CONTEXT

And the building of the wall of it was of jasper: and the city was pure gold, like unto clear glass. And the foundations of the wall of the city were garnished with all manner of precious stones. The first foundation was jasper; the second, sapphire; the third, a chalcedony; the fourth, an emerald; The fifth, sardonyx; the sixth, sardius; the seventh, chrysolyte; the eighth, beryl; the ninth, a topaz; the tenth, a chrysoprasus; the eleventh, a jacinth; the twelfth, an amethyst. And the twelve gates were twelve pearls; every several gate was of one pearl: and the street of the city was pure gold, as it were transparent glass. And I saw no temple therein: for the Lord God Almighty and the Lamb are the temple of it. **And the city had no need of the sun, neither of the moon, to shine in it: for the glory of God did lighten it, and the Lamb is the light thereof.** *And the nations of them which are saved shall walk in the light of it: and the kings of the earth do bring their glory and honour into it. And the gates of it shall not be shut at all by day: for there shall be no night there. And they shall bring the glory and honour of the nations into it. And there shall in no wise enter into it any thing that defileth, neither whatsoever worketh abomination, or maketh a lie: but they which are written in the Lamb's book of life.*

Rev 21:18-27

Gold, precious stone and pearls; they are all treasures today. In holy Jerusalem, they are construction materials. Exodus 39 describes a breastplate fashioned for the priest which included twelve precious stones symbolizing the twelve tribes of Israel. Gold and precious stones abound in the tabernacle God designed, but conspicuously absent are pearls. To a Jew the pearl is unclean, as are all shellfish, mussels and oyster products.

Pearls were highly prized by Egyptians. Greeks and Romans attributed them to the gods. In the middle east ancients called them tears of the gods. Pearls were gems of the gentiles.

The only other reference to a pearl in Scripture is the pearl of great price which was used to describe an attribute of the kingdom of heaven (Matt 13:45-46). When Peter had a vision of unclean things, he was told: "What God hath cleansed, that call not thou common" (Acts 11:8-9). He was being instructed to preach the gospel to the gentiles.

Clearly, God has made the pearl, the gentile, clean. We have all been made partakers of the glory of God. The only passport to holy Jerusalem is the Lamb's book of Life. Jew and gentile alike, all loved by God and all called to his salvation.

> *But glory, honour, and peace, to every man that worketh good, to the Jew first, and also to the Gentile: For there is no respect of persons with God.*　　　*Rom 2:10-11*

The temple of God was the place of his presence among men. It does not exist in holy Jerusalem. The presence of God is the very light of the city and the light of life today. It is his glory.

Dear Lord Jesus:

Show me your glory! It was Moses' request and my hope. You are the glory of God. Your Holy Spirit imparts that light into us who believe. Praise you, Lord, for being light that brightens our countenance. Praise you, Lord, for moving me from darkness into light. Forgive the darkness that still dwells in my flesh. Let your

light shine in my dark and shadowy places, so that I reflect your glory in my life. Thank you, Lord, for light and truth and hope.
Enlightened.

REFLECTION

In the morning, as it becoming light, I can see things that I knew were there, even in the darkness. Praise to God and to the Lamb who are there. I know and believe it. Someday there will be a fullness of the light so that I can see clearly. Doubts and shadows, even darkness exists today; but I know where my faith lives and what my hope contains. The night will be past and the day of shining forth will come. How marvelous it is to know that light is his glory, and that I can and will live in it.

PRACTICE:

I look into the deepest parts of my own life and see the unresolved darkness. Yet in this darkness there is light, the light of his glory. I look and see despair in the world, discouragement in the body of Christ and defeat in the lives of Christians. Yet in this darkness there is hope, the hope of his glory.

> *For God, who said, "Let light shine out of darkness," made his light shine in our hearts to give us the light of the knowledge of the glory of God in the face of Christ. 2 Cor 4:6*

How can I see his glory in all this darkness? By making a choice, by choosing to look into the face of believers and recognizing his face. After all, we are created in the image of God. When the vision of darkness seems overwhelming, the words "be true to the truth" rise up in my spirit. The truth is that his light shines out of our darkness. It is like a lighthouse shining in a stormy night. In the light we can see the glory of his saving grace.

It is the darkness in me that makes me unworthy; but it is the grace of his light that redeems me. It is this marvelous light that shows in my face and of those who believe and live in the truth. In his great mercy and wisdom he has provided for his manifest presence to be a practical experience. He has not forsaken me, nor rejected me, nor hidden the face of his glory from me. My heart cries out with the pain of life and its cry is to seek his face. I can practice seeing his glory. Knowing where to look, I now see his light everywhere.

> Practice being true to the truth, choose to focus on the light in your life and on the light in others. What cause for worship and praise. What a call to holy living.

50. Living Waters

And he shewed me a pure river of water of life, clear as
crystal, proceeding out of the throne of God and of the
Lamb. Rev 22:1

CONTEXT

*And he shewed me a pure river of water of life, clear as
crystal, proceeding out of the throne of God and of the
Lamb.* *In the midst of the street of it, and on either side of
the river, was there the tree of life, which bare twelve manner of fruits, and yielded her fruit every month: and the
leaves of the tree were for the healing of the nations.* *And
there shall be no more curse: but the throne of God and of
the Lamb shall be in it; and his servants shall serve him:
And they shall see his face; and his name shall be in their
foreheads.* *And there shall be no night there; and they
need no candle, neither light of the sun; for the Lord God
giveth them light: and they shall reign for ever and ever.
And he said unto me, These sayings are faithful and true:
and the Lord God of the holy prophets sent his angel to
shew unto his servants the things which must shortly be
done.* *Rev 22:1-6*

The Bible opens in a garden, and as it closes, the garden once
again appears. It was to be life-giving originally, and it will be
life-giving in eternity. The original garden included a river which
went out to water the garden. In the midst of the garden was the
tree of life and also that prohibited tree—the knowledge of good
and evil. Eden is revisited in the holy Jerusalem; the water of life
and the tree of life will bless for eternity, just as God intended.

Notice the difference between the river of living water and the
rivers of this fallen earth. God's river flows out, as did Eden's, and
is clear as crystal. Pure and holy because of its source, the living

213

God. Earthly rivers flow in; their contributories flow in and the river itself ultimately flows into the ocean. In the process, the river system takes life-giving nutrients from the earth through erosion. Man has made it even worse through pollution. The Mississippi is not only muddy, it's dangerous.

The river of life never fails to water, and the tree of life is never barren. Twelve fruits are produced continuously from month to month. There is both abundance and provision in the kingdom of heaven.

The real joy of holy Jerusalem, however, is the presence of God and our Savior, the Lamb. God told Moses, "no man shall see my face and live" (Ex 33:20), but we shall serve him and see his face. We shall live in the true and faithful light of his grace.

Dear Lord Jesus:

You are life today, Lord. I know someday the glory of a new creation, without a curse and in your presence, will come. It is my hope and it is based on your truth and your faithfulness. I live today with waters of life in me because of the Holy Spirit. Praise you, Lord, for the Holy Spirit which shows forth your love and life. Praise you, Lord, for light that can shine out of me and living waters of refreshing which can be shared. It is both a comfort and a challenge to live in your life today.

Well watered.

REFLECTION

It hasn't rained much this year and there are few wild flowers. The waters not only give life, they bring forth beauty. Both flowers and lives are meant to bloom and show the glory of God in their beauty. For the wild flowers it is the rain; for me it is the Holy Spirit. One is external and the other is internal. One is uncontrollable and the other is a choice. I can choose to let the Holy Spirit rain and reign in my life. It can flow in me and out from me. God

214

put the treasure of rain in the clouds and the treasure of his Holy Spirit in earthen vessels.

PRACTICE

> *Be astonished, O ye heavens, at this, and be horribly afraid, be ye very desolate, saith the LORD. For my people have committed two evils; they have forsaken me the fountain of living waters, and hewed them out cisterns, broken cisterns, that can hold no water.*
> *Jer 2:12-13*

We must recognize that life comes from God, and the substance of life is in God. It is not something that can be stored in cisterns, especially the broken cisterns of our sinful flesh. No, living water is meant to flow.

Jesus confused the woman at the well by speaking of living water. He calls it water that permanently quenches thirst and becomes *in him a well of water* (John 4:10-14). Later Jesus clarifies the matter by identifying this living water as the Holy Spirit.

> *He that believeth on me, as the scripture hath said, out of his belly shall flow rivers of living water. (But this spake he of the Spirit, which they that believe on him should receive: for the Holy Ghost was not yet given; because that Jesus was not yet glorified.)*
> *John 7:38-39*

There is an old spiritual song based on Psalm 46:4: *There is a river, the streams whereof shall make glad the city of God, the holy place of the tabernacles of the most High.*

I love the opening proclamation: *There's a river of life flowing out through me*, but the chorus is where practice is described. *Spring up, O well within my soul*; these are words we can speak and live. We can practice letting that river of life rise up and flow out through our lives. God intended it, Jesus made it possible, and the Holy Spirit enables it.

What should living water look like in our life? It is mourning with those who mourn and rejoicing with those who rejoice. It is speaking words of edification, encouragement, and enlightenment. It is comfort and the sacrifice of time to bless and care for one another. It is a hug, or even better, an embrace.

> Practice being a well of living water. Know the source of living water, and let it flow out through your life. A friend once told me God wants to pour his life into others through my life. Go and do likewise! Esteem and build up another person today. Do it with words and with the service of love.

51. Entering Obedience

Blessed are they that do his commandments, that they may have right to the tree of life, and may enter in through the gates into the city.   Rev 22:14

CONTEXT

Behold, I come quickly: blessed is he that keepeth the sayings of the prophecy of this book. And I John saw these things, and heard them. And when I had heard and seen, I fell down to worship before the feet of the angel which shewed me these things. Then saith he unto me, See thou do it not: for I am thy fellowservant, and of thy brethren the prophets, and of them which keep the sayings of this book: worship God. And he saith unto me, Seal not the sayings of the prophecy of this book: for the time is at hand. He that is unjust, let him be unjust still: and he which is filthy, let him be filthy still: and he that is righteous, let him be righteous still: and he that is holy, let him be holy still. And, behold, I come quickly; and my reward is with me, to give every man according as his work shall be. I am Alpha and Omega, the beginning and the end, the first and the last. **Blessed are they that do his commandments, that they may have right to the tree of life, and may enter in through the gates into the city.** *For without are dogs, and sorcerers, and whoremongers, and murderers, and idolaters, and whosoever loveth and maketh a lie. I Jesus have sent mine angel to testify unto you these things in the churches. I am the root and the offspring of David, and the bright and morning star.*   Rev 22:7-16

Revelation opens with a pronounced blessing for those who read, hear and keep its words. The blessing is reaffirmed as the book closes; for, having been read, and hopefully heard through

217

meditation, what remains is to keep its truths. A sense of urgency was expressed as the book opened and is reaffirmed with a reminder that the time is at hand. The urgency is strengthened in our Lord's declaration of coming quickly. Nearly 2000 years later, the urgency is not lessened. The time is at hand; he is coming quickly, and in some points of view he has come, certainly in the lives of those who are called by his name.

John is chastened when he worships the messenger, being told to worship God. This is not a casual issue today; it seems that we often worship those who bring us the word of God. It is only God who deserves worship. He alone has redeemed us, and he alone is worthy of our worship.

The book is not to be sealed; it is left open as a revelation, not as a mystery. It is a book that not only can be understood—it can be lived. We can deny the calling and continue to live sinful lives; or we can choose to let God do his perfect work in our lives. It has always been a choice, from the garden through today, and into tomorrow. It is Jesus who fills the garden and the city of God; he is Alpha and Omega.

Moses made our choice exceptionally clear:

> *I call heaven and earth to record this day against you, that I have set before you life and death, blessing and cursing: therefore choose life, that both thou and thy seed may live: That thou mayest love the LORD thy God, and that thou mayest obey his voice, and that thou mayest cleave unto him: for he is thy life,*   *Deut 30:19-20a*

The issue is obedience: it is a choice to believe; it is a choice to repent; it is a choice to walk in holiness, and it is a choice to enter his blessing. The tree of life was kept from Adam and Eve so that redemption would be possible. The tree of life is given to us; it is eternal and it is lavish beyond anything we can think or imagine.

Dear Lord Jesus:

Entering in is your calling for me, Lord. Help me to obey not only your commandment to love, but to enter in to your calling. You have the keys to life, Lord. In you I find joy and also significance and security. It is grace and peace to me, Lord. Thank you for paying the price so that I might enter. There is life in you; there is fulness in you; there is all I ever need in you. Praise you, Lord, for making it possible to obey. It is a struggle, but your Holy Spirit is my overcoming strength.

Entering in.

REFLECTION

Praise is something to be entered into. His joy is also a choice. Adam and Eve had a choice; and I have a choice. They erred and I have extended their error in so many ways. Thankfully, my God has provided for both redemption and for restoration. Praise to my God and savior, I can still choose to enter his obedience and his kingdom. I am not alone; he has given me his Word for warning and for reward. He has given me his Holy Spirit to convict and encourage. His body builds me up and helps me to walk in his ways. Praise him, I have all that is needed for life and godliness.

PRACTICE

What does it mean to do his commandments? Does it mean we must be careful to eat certain foods, be sure we rest on the Sabbath, not touch dead things or honor a host of other rules and regulations?

The Pharisees were great at rule keeping, but Jesus called them whited sepulchers and a host of other undistinguished titles. No, obedience is not found in legalism, which leads to bondage. God has given us liberty.

Micah tells us what God requires: "to do justly, and to love mercy, and to walk humbly with thy God" (Micah 6:8b). Jesus tells us to love God wholly and to love our neighbor as our self. He told Peter over breakfast that his love would be reflected by feeding his sheep (John 21:16). Does that mean we all need to be preachers or missionaries? Vocationally, probably not, but as a part of the body of Christ, certainly. It simply means to care. It means to look for opportunities to help, to encourage and to edify.

I love the word, esteem; it seems to summarize how we can relate to one another in holiness. We can exercise the power of esteeming by speaking highly of someone in their presence. Tell someone what great value they are to you in life.

Two steps are required for this exercise. First, you must involve yourself in relationships. To express value, there must be value and it must be real, not just words. Secondly, you must actually express value to the individual.

Start this practice with those who are close, but open it to those whom you must purpose to find and esteem. One idea is to think of someone who had an impact in your life and whom you haven't seen for a while. Call them, or better yet write them, tell them how much they added to your life.

52. Come to Him

And the Spirit and the bride say, Come. And let him that
heareth say, Come. And let him that is athirst come. And
whosoever will, let him take the water of life freely.

Rev 22:17

CONTEXT

*And the Spirit and the bride say, Come. And let him that
heareth say, Come. And let him that is athirst come. And
whosoever will, let him take the water of life freely. For I
testify unto every man that heareth the words of the prophecy of this book, If any man shall add unto these things,
God shall add unto him the plagues that are written in this
book: And if any man shall take away from the words of
the book of this prophecy, God shall take away his part out
of the book of life, and out of the holy city, and from the
things which are written in this book. He which testifieth
these things saith, Surely I come quickly. Amen. Even so,
come, Lord Jesus. The grace of our Lord Jesus Christ be
with you all. Amen.* Rev 22:17-21

What an invitation! The waters of life are freely available, yet
so few seem to come. Are they not thirsty? Surely there is a great
thirst. Marketers know of the human thirst and scream of products
that promise to give life gusto. The result is a headache and often
an addiction to come to the dryness of gusto again and again. The
world is starving for living waters, but even in its midst they do not
drink. Perhaps they cannot, or will not, hear the call to come. It is
more likely they do not come because the Spirit and the bride do
not say come. Where is the Spirit except in the body of Christ?
Some of the last words of our Lord were:

221

But ye shall receive power, after that the Holy Ghost is come upon you: and ye shall be witnesses unto me both in Jerusalem, and in all Judaea, and in Samaria, and unto the uttermost part of the earth.   Acts 1:8

The plethora of preachers and missionaries, together with incredible advances in communication technology, certainly would get the message out. Again, perhaps they do not come because the Spirit and the bride do not say come. The key may be in the word, "and." It may be a lack of unity. When the spirit and the bride say the same thing, then the words will have the power promised in Jesus' last words.

Disunity becomes apparent in adding to and taking away from the words God has given. Except for politics, perhaps the easiest thing to argue about is religion. Seeing the strife and conflict over religion, one could believe it was a fulfillment of the words: *God shall add unto him the plagues that are written in this book.* Let us seek unity, and in the seeking be careful with the Word of God. Those are the words which enable the Spirit and the bride to say the same thing—come.

The Revelation concludes with a promise of his return and a benediction of grace. They are established with an Amen. We must not minimize the power of our words: in them are both life and death. The grace of our Lord Jesus Christ is for all. Give it life with words of amen; an amen that is more than just a word, but a lifestyle.

Dear Lord Jesus:

How easy it is to miss the point in your Word. I always thought of this verse as hastening your return. No, it is an invitation to those who will come. This is a verse for today, not a future hope. Praise you, Lord, for being a living presence today. Lord, keep me from taking your word out of context. Thank you, Lord, that you are coming in glory; but even more, you are here in Spirit. Help me to be one that hears and one that speaks, in unity with the Holy

Spirit, saying, "Come!" Help me say it to my neighbor and to my family. Help me say it to those whom you send through my life. Help me to come and drink of your living water: it is life.
Thirsty.

REFLECTION

The waters of life seem scarce, but in reality they are plentiful and available. In my flesh I look to circumstance to find life, but it is not there. The Word and the world both promise circumstantial problems in life, but living water is independent of circumstance. There are many testimonies of grace under fire and of joy within despair which show that true life is not found in circumstance. Living water is something to come to; it is not just everywhere. I must come to my Lord and savior, Jesus Christ; he gives living water and restores me in love and life. He has the words of life which lead me to the waters of life. I love him with his love, out of his life and love in me.

PRACTICE

In the world and in the church we seem to be focused on circumstance. A survey of prayer requests at my church, and I know at many others, is almost exclusively circumstantial. Mostly they are concerned with health or other physical needs. The prayer requests represent real and present needs; they are the expression of our heart's desire and of God's promised provision. After all, we live among our circumstances. Fortunately, life is not about our circumstances; at least not the life that living water nourishes.

The key to saying the same thing as the Spirit of God is in recognizing the unifier. Unity, unfortunately, is also often seen as circumstantial. Articles on unity in the church often focus on differences in form. How we baptize, pray, order our worship services, or otherwise choose to express ourselves becomes the very definition of unity, or more appropriately, disunity. We don't realize that within this very diversity is where unity is found. Paul clearly points to diversity as being what makes the body of Christ a unity, and chastens us for letting differences bring disunity (1 Cor 12).

Learn to rejoice in unity; then the Spirit and the bride will say come. The invitation to come will be to people, saying come to the one who gives living water. Then we can look for that blessed hope, and the glorious appearing of the great God and our Savior, Jesus Christ (Titus 2:13).

To practice unity in the body, find a friend (one with a different background, a different denomination) and go to lunch together. Make sure your friend expects to talk about spiritual things and be open to discover how your differences add to the body of Christ. Talk about spiritual gifts and how their diversity draws unbelievers and edifies believers.

APPENDIX

The Form and Practice of Meditation

Very often spiritual disciplines encouraged in the Word of God are neglected simply because we don't know how to exercise them. In the physical world, things that do not come naturally must be learned and exercised. Somehow we all learn to walk and talk by doing what comes naturally. However, if we want to swim we have to be learn how and practice it. If we want to swim well we might even take lessons. If we want to be excellent, we might get a coach and work out, as well as practice proper strokes.

Spiritual disciplines are as unnatural to our flesh as is swimming. The disciples asked Jesus to teach them to pray and he did not rebuke them, he taught them by word and by example. We can learn to pray and we can learn to meditate, but like swimming, the benefits will come from actual practice. Meditation is purposed by God to be experienced, to be a personal discipline. The blessings from meditation, promised in Scripture, are individual and personal.

In swimming there are many different strokes; individually we may be better at some strokes. In like manner, there are many ways to meditate on the Word. All of them are beneficial, but some may be more appropriate to our individual aptitude and desire.

Regardless of method or form, there are principles which always apply. Some of the more important general principles include:

> **Context:** It is important to stay in context. Do not be tempted to drift into other related or even unrelated matters. Scripture is always a consistent message. Even small passages have a context, and that needs to be the framework of our meditation.

225

Focus: Meditation is designed by God to be specific. It is easy to be so broad that any life application becomes too general, and we lose the opportunity to practice what the Holy Spirit shows us. Only one idea or theme should be the focus of a meditation. You will be surprised how much can come out of a single idea.

Expression: For a meditation to become life, it must be expressed. Write your meditation. Talk to others about it in small groups or with your family. Finally, live the meditation. Let the expression become life through practice.

VERSE MEDITATION

The most common approach to meditation is to read a selected passage several times, pick a verse and simply think about it. It is more than just thinking, however, it is hearing what the Holy Spirit says in our heart and then keeping the words in our daily life. Verse meditation is the method used in this book, which is described in more detail in the Introduction.

LARGE PASSAGE MEDITATION

Large passages of scripture can also serve as food for meditation. Consider the lengthy prayers expressed in Daniel 9 and Nehemiah 9. Just reading these words reveals the breadth, length and height of God's works and ways. His name and his character is described in glorious terms, and the reality of his person is recounted by remembering our heritage and his faithfulness in specific terms.

When large passages are used, it is important not to be too broad. Meditation is designed to be focused. For example, the prayers in Daniel or Nehemiah could be used to focus on the character of God. Consider just listing and thinking about his character as you read the prayers. Psalm 19 or 119 might also be a good place for large passage meditation. In these passages the focus would be the Word of God. The meditation would focus on the breadth and height of specific attributes of the Word of God.

THEMATIC MEDITATION

A variation on large passage meditation is thematic meditation. This method requires a little homework prior to engaging in meditation. The practice is to select a specific topic and gather a number of verses relating to the topic, being careful not to take them out of context. Even though many scriptures have been committed to memory, a concordance or topical bible is often useful for this work. One could, for example, gather a number of verses on faithfulness and link them together topically.

Consider the following:

> *Thy testimonies that thou hast commanded are righteous and very faithful.*   *Ps 119:138*

> *If we confess our sins, he is faithful and just to forgive us our sins, and to cleanse us from all unrighteousness.*
> *I Jn 1:9*

> *Let us hold fast the profession of our faith without wavering; (for he is faithful that promised;)*   *Heb 10:23*

> *Being confident of this very thing, that he which hath begun a good work in you will perform it until the day of Jesus Christ:*   *Phil 1:6*

> *But the Lord is faithful, who shall stablish you, and keep you from evil.*   *II Th 3:3*

> *It is of the LORD's mercies that we are not consumed, because his compassions fail not. They are new every morning: great is thy faithfulness.*   *Lam 3:22-23*

Notice that the verses on faithfulness are not just random, they are ordered in a manner that flows together thematically. They recognize his faithfulness, acknowledge our failure, profess the resolution, and result in praise.

With the homework done, the theme of faithfulness can then be the focus of meditation. For those who are musically inclined, the words of great hymns such as *Great Is Thy Faithfulness* may be useful supplements to this meditation. Meditation can surely lead to worship and hymns become a natural affirmation of God's faithfulness.

WORD BY WORD MEDITATION

Because meditation is designed to be focused, the tightest approach would be to meditate on single words in Scripture. This approach is not common but may have some of the greatest potential—finding life in every word God has spoken.

> *... that he might make thee know that man doth not live by bread only, but by every word that proceedeth out of the mouth of the LORD doth man live.*   *Deut 8:3b*

The word of God is rich in breadth but also infinite in depth. Large passages of scripture certainly recount his glory and give him praise, but single verses can produce similar results. Even the words within a verse can become seeds for powerful meditation.

Jesus countered the tempter's challenge to turn stones to bread with the words: "*It is written: 'Man does not live on bread alone, but on every word that comes from the mouth of God.'*" (Matt 4:4). Jesus also stressed the importance of jots and tittles (Matt 5:18), underscoring the smallest details of God's Word.

To understand the word by word approach, consider each word of a common verse, one so well known familiarity often weakens the power of its message.

The LORD is my shepherd; ...   Psalm 23:1a

The LORD is my shepherd: Consider the singularity of
God. He is One. He is both the unity of the godhead and
the primacy of creation. There is none like him, only he is
God.

*The **LORD** is my shepherd:* He is Lord! All authority
and power is given to him. By him were all things created;
and we are his servants, even in our rebellious times. I can
learn to worship by seeing the awesome glory of his lordship. Like Isaiah, I must declare, "Woe is me," when I see
him. But he touches me and then I can say, "Here am I
send Me" (Isaiah 6:5,8).

*The LORD **is** my shepherd:* He is not an absentee God, he
is present. His presence is known in his creation and in
our lives. He has given us the Holy Spirit so that we can
know him and sense his nearness. He is, and calls himself
"I AM THAT I AM" (Exodus 3:14).

*The LORD is **my** shepherd :* He is personal. He loves me
with his love. He wants my salvation to be matured and
for me to be restored to close fellowship with himself. He
loves the world, but he also loves me and wants to call me
his friend.

*The LORD is my **shepherd**:* The beauty of his presence
is that it is for my good. He leads and directs when I ask.
He chastens and corrects when I choose rebellion or igno-
rance. He is purposed to complete the good work he began in me (Phil 1:6).

These little reflections on the depth of each word only begin to
work out its scope. Every word in the twenty-third Psalm leads us
to behold his person. Through word by word meditation we can
live the balance of the opening verse: "I shall not want."

In this way Scripture is found to be truly infinite, enabling us to meditate considering large passages or the smallest detail. Consider a favorite Sunday School memory verse:

Jesus wept.   *John 11:35*

> **Jesus** *wept*: Consider the name of Jesus. Mary was told to give him this name because he will save His people from their sins. In the name of Jesus I find power and authority to live a godly life. I even pray in Jesus' name.
>
> *Jesus* **wept**: What makes my Savior weep? How have I broken his heart today? Is there some way that I can weep with him—to share his pain? The response to seeing Jesus weep was, "see how he loved him" (vs. 36). Can my tears also become a testimony of love, his love?

CANT SLEEP? MEDITATE!

Several years ago pressures of life were high, and I found myself waking in the night, unable to go back to sleep. The world says to count sheep when this happens. God said to consider my Shepherd. Psalm 23 became the verse of my night watches, and word by word meditation the pathway to rest. I would recite the verse considering each word. Very often I would not get past "The Lord is my ..." and sleep would come. The meditation would become life, my anxiety would flee and "I shall not want" became fulfilled in rest.

I am older now, and night watches come for other reasons, but I still choose to meditate word for word till rest returns. I pray that in my final sleep I will awaken to the reality of his presence, a nearness that is currently being experienced in the meditations of my heart.

EXTENDING THE PRINCIPLE

Although the practice of word by word meditation is primarily a personal discipline, the approach is equally valid as a small group exercise. Our appreciation for the depth of God's word is fortified as we hear others consider each word and share its depth of meaning for them personally. Sharing word by word meditation seems non-threatening; it is a way to allow those who have limited Biblical knowledge to share in its truth and application to life.

My meditation of him shall be sweet:
I will be glad in the LORD.

Psalm 104:34